Primary school design

Primary school design

Malcolm Seaborne
Principal, Chester College

Routledge & Kegan Paul   London

First published 1971
by Routledge & Kegan Paul Ltd
Broadway House, 68-74 Carter Lane
London EC4V 5EL
Printed in Great Britain by
Northumberland Press Ltd
Gateshead 8
© Malcolm Seaborne 1971

ISBN 0 7100 7075 6

Contents

Figures in text

Preface

This short study of primary school buildings is based upon visits made to a large number of primary schools in different parts of the country. In writing up these visits, I have adopted a case-study approach and made what I hope is a representative selection of schools of various types and dates. My aim has been to open up questions relating to primary school design for more general discussion, by showing the relevance of past experience to present problems and by sampling the views of teachers and architects. The names of the particular schools dealt with have not been given but I should like to record my appreciation of the friendliness and candour shown by the teachers and architects with whom I discussed the questions raised in the following study. I am especially grateful to the architects who lent the plans included in this book andto Mr G. Rigby who redrew them for publication.

This book was written when I was on the staff of Leicester University School of Education. I am grateful to a number of mature students who made observations about their school buildings, and to my former colleague, Mr Eric Davies, with whom I also had some very useful discussions. I am indebted to Mr Brian Burch for help with the proofs.

Finally, I should like to thank the Leverhulme Trust for making a grant to cover the travelling and other expenses incurred in writing this book, which forms part of a wider study of the development of school architecture and organization.

M.S.

1 Primary school buildings today

The importance of the environment

The importance attached to the physical environment of learning has varied considerably from one educationist to another. Edward Thring, the Victorian headmaster of Uppingham School, considered that 'the permanent conditions under which work has to be done' – what he called 'the almighty wall' – was 'the supreme and final arbiter of schools'. He spoke with great feeling because the new school buildings erected at Uppingham during his period as headmaster were financed with great sacrifice by himself and members of his staff. Nowadays the Exchequer and the L.E.A.s provide most of the money needed for new school buildings and except in the independent and voluntary school sectors, people are perhaps less generally aware of the financial aspect of new school provision. It may be that for this reason we also sometimes undervalue the importance of school architecture for securing the conditions needed for effective teaching.

It is probable that Thring overestimated the importance of his school buildings, but it is all too easy to adopt the attitude that it is not the buildings but the teachers who really count in education. One over-modest school architect with whom this point was discussed estimated that the ability of the teacher accounts for ninety-nine per cent and the building for only one per cent of a school's effectiveness. But some teachers at least take a different view. A teacher in a recently-built primary school said in discussion that in his experience 'the building made the teaching method' and mentioned that he has warned an architect friend of his to 'be careful' because what the architect plans, the teacher has to live with.

Teachers and children are almost certainly much more influenced by their physical environment than they often realize, at any rate consciously. Teachers are used to adapting their teaching material to the varying ages and abilities of the children, and it may be that for an analogous reason they are more than usually ready to adapt an unsuitable building to the methods of teaching they prefer. Certainly one admires the way that teachers in worn-out old buildings nevertheless often manage to teach effectively, and it is also true that children are remarkably resilient and can be happy whatever the building is like. This, however, is to miss the point. It is a severe drain on the energies of teachers to have to be constantly improvising to make an unsuitable building work. It also has to be recognized that some schools are basically of such bad design that no amount of improvisation will enable the staff to teach the children in the best possible way.

Main types of building

It is too easily assumed that the older the building is, the more difficult it will be to use modern teaching methods. This may well be broadly true but a more crucial criterion is often the amount of floor area available in relation to the number of children in the school. Good modern furniture and equipment can also make a great deal of difference. There are certainly some schools of nineteenth-century date or even earlier where, because the school population in the area has declined, there is plenty of space (to do practical work for example), and enough equipment for the teacher to use a variety of methods. Equally, there are schools of the latest design which are seriously overcrowded and hence frustrate many of the teachers' aims. This book is an attempt to consider the broad categories of primary schools built over the last hundred years and to estimate to what extent they are being successfully adapted to modern teaching methods. Naturally we must take account of the human factor as well as the architectural. There will always be some teachers who can do interesting work in the most unpromising surroundings and others who remain uninspiring in spite of being given every modern facility. Nevertheless, it is hoped that a general picture can be given which will have some validity in spite of the individual exceptions which are bound to exist.

We will find that the earliest schools consisted simply of one schoolroom. Later, classrooms were added and by the end of the nineteenth century it was usual to arrange them around a central hall. Then in the twentieth century veranda schools made their appearance followed by schools arranged around open quadrangles or with classrooms served by long corridors. Since the Second World War the corridor plans have been replaced by more compact designs leading to the present move towards open planning.

Consultation and control

Before a primary school is built today there are full consultations between the administrative officers of the education committee, the architect, the educational advisers and (more often than hitherto)

practising teachers. The plans of new schools are frequently discussed in the educational and architectural press, and the Department of Education and Science (which has to approve all new school
plans) also puts its point of view. Ever since Exchequer funds began
to be used for educational building after 1833, school plans have been
subject to approval by the Government, and since the Second World
War the architects' and buildings branch of the Department of Education and Science has done much to influence school design by
issuing Building Bulletins and entering into close consultation with
local authorities. The controls exercised by the Government have
aptly been called the 'floor' and the 'ceiling' of any new school project. The 'floor' is the insistence on a minimum number of square feet
of teaching area per child, and other minimum standards laid down
in the official Building Regulations, such as the number of wash-
basins and toilets to be provided, the area of playground, playing
fields and so on. The 'ceiling' is the cost limit, calculated on so much
for each child, an amount which is varied from time to time according to the level of prices.

Thus L.E.A.s are free to design and build schools subject to the
current Building Regulations and cost-place limits, and of course
subject to satisfying the Government that a new school really is
needed in a particular area. Until very recently, new primary schools
could only be built when they were needed to provide places for the
growing school population, or because a large number of children
had moved into the area. Money was not available simply for replacing old buildings, although it often happened that the building
of a new school made it possible to close or at least reduce the numbers in adjoining older buildings. In 1970, however, it was announced that in future money may be spent on replacing out-of-date
primary school buildings and though, as we shall see, there is much
leeway to be made up, the change of policy has given new hope to
those working in the primary school field.

The need for follow-up studies

The consultation which takes place before a new primary school is
built is therefore considerable. L.E.A.s vary a good deal in the
amount of trouble they take to consult practising teachers, but in
recent years there has probably been some improvement in this
respect. What still seems to be lacking is any systematic attempt to
estimate the efficiency of the school building once it has been actually

constructed and occupied. It is usual to have a 'hand-over meeting' about six months after completion at which any structural defects are pointed out to the contractor, who is legally obliged to remedy them. But it is too late at that juncture to attempt to remedy any faults in the basic design which may have become apparent. Opinion about the suitability of a building depends to a considerable extent on the teaching methods being used, while such matters as the colour scheme chosen for decoration, the amount of light and ventilation provided and so on are often of a subjective character about which it is difficult to find agreement. Nevertheless, it can certainly be argued that too few attempts have been made to obtain 'consumer reaction' from teachers and children actually using the building. Nor have teachers always been made sufficiently aware of the design problems faced by the architects (e.g. the difficulties presented by a sloping site) or of the educational aims which determined the brief given to the architects in the first place.

And here we meet one of the most interesting aspects of school design, namely the question of how far it is possible or desirable for educationists and architects to manipulate the environment so as to encourage or even force the adoption of certain approved teaching methods. It sometimes happens that a building has been designed with certain educational aims in mind and the teachers who actually use the building may be doing their best to frustrate them. For example, in one school visited, each classroom had intentionally been designed without a focal point where the teacher could stand and there was no fixed chalk-board to confirm the teacher in his role as an expositor. In spite of that, the teacher had fixed a large piece of brown paper to the wall and was chalking on it while giving a formal lesson. In another case, two classrooms were separated from each other by wide openings instead of doors in order to encourage the two teachers to share the resources of both rooms, but furniture had been moved in an attempt to isolate the one class from the other.

Now there is nothing necessarily reprehensible, or indeed new, in frustrating an architect's design in ways like these. The desire to alter the environment, which we may condemn in a situation where traditional habits are struggling to maintain themselves, might not be condemned, for example, in an old school where a teacher was somehow or other managing to introduce new ideas and altering the position of the furniture in order to do so. The important point for our purpose is to recognize what the architecture was designed to do and which teaching methods are being used so that we can better study their inevitable interaction.

The design element

It may be argued that the architecture of a school building should not be used in an attempt to dictate the teaching methods employed. Any structure, however, is bound to create a certain environment: even one large space, which might appear to give the teachers the maximum possible freedom to vary their methods, would in reality be built with that purpose (with which not all would agree) in mind and would also effectively prevent the adoption of certain types of teaching. Similarly the amount of light and heat provided, the kind of decoration, floor-finish and so on would all have their effect on the environment created. In actual fact, we find that the schools in use today but built at various times in the past were all designed with certain educational and architectural aims in mind. At some periods the architectural aspect has overwhelmed the educational – as, for example, where a school built in the 1840s (and still in use today) was given lancet windows of perfect Gothic design without apparently taking account of the lack of natural light inside the building which resulted. Conversely, some would argue that in the 1960s too much glass was provided in schools, partly at least because of the architectural ideas then current.

In general, however, school buildings, and particularly elementary or primary schools, have always taken close account of their functional purpose: very rarely has sufficient money been available to spend on architectural embellishments. Thus it is possible to study changing educational ideas and teaching methods through the sequence of buildings and such a study is a valuable supplement to what can be learnt from purely written sources. It is vital to remember that the plans which we will be considering, however outdated they are now, were accepted at the time as the most suitable for the type of education then provided. The questions we therefore have to ask ourselves are: what was the original rationale of the building? and, how far can the building still be used effectively even though the rationale has changed?

The educational component

By the rationale of a building is meant the pattern of internal organization and the teaching methods for which the building was originally designed. Clearly this educational component has varied considerably since mass education was introduced during the nineteenth century and many new elementary schools began to be built. But methods of teaching and organization, though they have developed over the years, have not changed in a uniform or continuous manner. There are still teachers who at least for part of the time use methods which gained acceptance many years ago, and occasionally one finds that what appears to be a new approach is in fact a much older one in a revised form. Group work, for example, which is now widespread in modern primary schools, was a feature of the monitorial schools of the early nineteenth century, albeit in a very different form. Similarly, the common practices of the Victorian period of learning passages of poetry by heart and chanting multiplication tables have not entirely disappeared from the schools and are still considered by some teachers to have educational value. Nevertheless, certain broad trends may be discerned and this book will deal with some of the principal changes which have taken place in teaching methods as well as buildings.

So far as the internal organization of the school is concerned, the degree of responsibility given to heads of schools, assistant teachers and the children themselves are the variables which need to be considered. The size of the class unit is also of obvious importance. Why has a teacher/pupil ratio of 1/40 been accepted since the Second World War, with even larger numbers before that? Why has a new drive to reduce primary classes to thirty begun in the 1970s? Is there any special significance in such numbers, or have they varied simply with the amount of money available to spend on the employment of teachers and the provision of rooms suited to classes of a pre-determined size? So too, the organization within the classroom has changed from time to time and may vary from school to school at any given date. When, and for what reasons, has the emphasis been placed on teaching the children as a class, or in groups, or individually? In spite of these variables, however, general tendencies are apparent which are reflected in the types of school buildings provided over the last century.

The condition of primary school buildings

In the last few years, more attention has been paid to the physical condition of our existing primary schools. In 1962 the National Union of Teachers carried out a survey which was published in January 1963 under the title of *The state of our schools*. Of the primary schools sampled, 41 per cent were without a separate staff-room, 44 per cent had no hall and 60 per cent were without a separate dining room. In addition, half the schools did not possess a playing field. Other details were given of toilet facilities (frequently inadequate) and of the provision of equipment, which varied from 92 per cent of the schools possessing a piano to only 4 per cent with a television set. Also in 1963, as part of the Campaign for Education, a booklet, *School Building. A Survey of the Present Programme and its Limitations*, was issued which attacked the Government for the inadequacy of the school-building programme and quoted many instances of shockingly inadequate primary school buildings. In the meantime, and no doubt as a result of growing public pressure, the Government undertook a detailed survey of maintained school buildings which was carried out by the Department of Education and Science in 1962 and published three years later as *The School Building Survey*. Table I, which is based on information given in this survey, lists some of the major defects discovered in primary school buildings as a result of this enquiry.

Table I   *Major defects in primary school accommodation in England and Wales, 1962*

	No. of schools	Percentage of total
Sanitation mainly out of doors	15,441	66·5
Seriously sub-standard site[a]	9,211	39·7
No staffroom	8,750	37·7
No warm water supply for pupils	6,101	26·3
No central heating system	5,815	25·1
No kitchen or scullery on site	4,647	20·0
No hall[b]	4,073	17·6
Dining in classrooms[b]	2,288	9·9

[a] i.e. with less than two-thirds of the area prescribed in the 1959 Building Regulations (excluding playing fields).
[b] Excluding primary schools for less than 100 pupils.

The cost of remedying the worst defects was estimated in 1967 to be in the region of £70 million. Hardly a week passes without some reference in the Press to inadequate primary school buildings and both the main political parties in the 1970 General Election Campaign promised to give this question urgent attention.

Main periods of building

How out of date, or to be more impartial, exactly how old are our primary school buildings? The Government survey of 1962 classified maintained schools according to the age of the oldest main building still in use, with the results shown in Table II.

Table II Age of maintained primary school buildings in England and Wales, 1962

Age of oldest main building	County schools	Voluntary schools	Total
Pre-1875	1,809	5,345	7,154
1875-1902	4,390	2,349	6,739
1903-1918	2,483	500	2,983
1919-1944	2,221	438	2,659
1945-1962	3,064	606	3,670
	13,967	9,238	23,205

It will be seen that well over half of the total number of primary schools still in use in 1962 were built before 1903. The majority of the nineteenth-century schools were voluntary or Church schools, as one would expect when one recalls that before the 1870 Education Act virtually all primary school building was in the hands of voluntary societies, particularly the National Society associated with the Church of England. It has to be remembered, however, that many of the nineteenth-century primary schools still in use are small country schools, so that the percentage of pupils in old buildings is not as great as one might imagine from the information given above. Table III makes this clear but, even so, some 44 per cent of primary school children were in pre-1903 schools in 1962.

Table III Percentage of pupils in primary schools of varying date

Age of oldest main building	Percentage of schools	Percentage of pupils
Pre-1875	30·8	18·7
1875-1902	29·0	25·5
1903-1918	12·9	14·8
1919-1944	11·5	17·0
1945-1962	15·8	24·0

It is difficult to say exactly how far the picture given in the survey of 1962 has been modified by new building since that date. The primary school building programme is being stepped up but much of the new building since 1962 has been to provide accommodation for additional pupils, which has sometimes, but not always, made it possible to close old schools. The Plowden Report of 1967 (*Children and their Primary Schools*, ch. 28) was obliged to accept the statistics given in the 1962 Government survey of English and Welsh schools as the best available, the apparent differences in the figures given in the Plowden Report being accounted for by the exclusion of those relating to Wales (where the state of the primary schools was separately examined in the Gittins Report, *Primary Education in Wales*, 1967, ch. 26).

In an attempt to provide a more detailed and up-to-date picture, at any rate in one sample area, an analysis of the dates of school buildings in use in an adjoining city and county was made in 1970, with the result shown in Table IV.

Though the situation in this area may not be typical of all parts of the country the following points arising from Table IV are probably of general application. In the first place, the marked contrast between the city and county areas in the number of schools built during the nineteenth century is not as significant as might at first appear since, as we have seen, country schools are usually much smaller than those in the towns. We also need to remember that the immediate surroundings of the country schools are often pleasant and that much has been done in recent years to improve the amenities of the older rural schools. Secondly, although the oldest schools still in use are now mainly in the countryside, the first elementary schools erected as a result of the enormous increase in population brought by the Industrial Revolution were generally built in the towns early in the nineteenth century and were replaced after 1870 by Board schools, most of which were very large and are still in use. The main drive in rural elementary school building began, as the Table indicates, in the 1840s, and rose to a peak following the passing of the 1870 Education Act. Many of these schools have remained in use because there has been more space than in the towns for extensions, and the thinner scatter of population in the country has always made it essential to have a substantial number of small schools. The number of such schools has been gradually reduced since about 1900, chiefly because of improvements in transport which have made it possible to amalgamate small schools.

Table IV   Sample area: number and dates of primary school buildings in use in 1970

Period built	City schools	County schools
1800-09	—	1
1810-19	—	3
1820-29	—	1
1830-39	—	6
1840-49	—	18
1850-59	—	18
1860-69	1	17
1870-79	6	30
1880-89	13	10
1890-99	10	9
Nineteenth century	30	113
1900-09	2	16
1910-19	2	4
1920-29	7	5
1930-39	22	14
1940-49	2	—
1950-59	28	11
1960-69	6	40
Twentieth century	69	90
Totals	99	203[a]

[a] Two of the county schools dated from before 1800 and a further 45 could not be dated accurately and are therefore excluded. (They belong in fact mainly to the nineteenth century.)

A further general historical development which is reflected in Table IV is the fact that after about 1900 there was a decline in the birth-rate so that in the city area noted here, for example, the education committee set up under the 1902 Education Act was on the whole able to manage with the new schools built by the School Board before 1902. The county authority, on the other hand, had rather more leeway to make up during the first decade of the twentieth century because of the poor state of many of the rural voluntary schools by that date. During the second and third decades of the twentieth century there was a slackening in the rate of primary school building because of the First World War and the greater attention given to secondary schools following the passing of the 1902 and 1918 Education Acts. In the 1930s there was a notable increase in the rate of primary school building as a byproduct of the policy of rehousing families from the city centres in new housing estates, a policy which naturally had less marked results in most county areas.

Since the Second World War there has been a considerable amount of new building in both city and county areas. It will be seen from Table IV that the peak came in the 1950s in the sample city area and in the 1960s in the county. One possible interpretation is to suggest that in the 1950s the city was mainly preoccupied with the immediate post-war 'bulge', during which period also a number of new housing estates were being built. The county, on the other hand, with more space available in its existing primary school buildings, was able to concentrate on the new secondary schools needed to implement its plans for secondary school reorganization, after which more attention was paid to the primary school sector.

It will be sufficiently clear from the Tables given in this chapter that the various phases of primary school building may be related to the important Education Acts which were passed in 1870, 1902, 1918 and 1944. It is with this general background in mind that we now turn to consider the main types of plan used in building primary schools over approximately the last hundred years, and to study a selection of actual schools of varying date which are still in use today.

Note

There were in 1962 some 14,000 nineteenth-century primary schools in existence (see Table II). About 2,000 of these were closed between 1962 and 1970, and many of the remainder have either been improved or are not considered to be worth replacing. In October 1970 the Secretary of State for Education and Science announced the allocation of £38 million in the school building programme for 1972-3 to replace or improve about 500 of the 3,000 primary schools built before 1903 'which are deficient in teaching area and in ancillary accommodation or amenities, and whose replacement or improvement is justified because of long-term need for the accommodation'. The

Secretary of State also hoped that the rest of these 3,000 seriously substandard schools would be replaced or modernized before 1977, by further allocations of money in future school building programmes. The latest official estimate (April 1971) is that between 6,000 and 6,500 pre-1903 primary schools need replacement or improvement.

2 The one-room plan and its derivatives

Early plans

When the problem of mass elementary education was first faced in the early nineteenth century educationists inevitably took as their model the type of schoolroom which had been usual in England since the later Middle Ages. The original schoolroom at Winchester, as at Eton, Harrow and other less famous schools, consisted simply of one very large room, in various parts of which the forms were taught by a number of assistant masters or 'ushers'. Qualified assistants could not be afforded for the new elementary schools of the early nineteenth century and monitors were employed to take groups of children under the supervision of a single master or mistress. Joseph Lancaster's plan for a school of 320 children consisted of a room measuring 70 by 32 feet, which gave each child 7 square feet, but the monitorial schools more usually allowed 6 square feet per child. In the Lancasterian schools long desks and benches were arranged in the main body of the room to face the master, with aisles at the sides so that the children, when not at their desks, could stand in semi-circles facing the side walls, on which lesson-boards were hung. Writing was done at the desks and reading facing the wall.

The early National school plans resembled the Lancasterian in accommodating all the children in one large room but the main body of the room was taken up with groups of movable benches, each occupied by a class of about a dozen children under a monitor. These were the reading groups, the writing being done at desks facing the side walls, i.e. the reverse of the Lancasterian system. Another important innovation was introduced by Wilderspin and Stow, initially in infant schools only, but later in schools for older children as well. This was the gallery, which consisted of a stepped floor on which the children sat. These galleries were used entirely for oral lessons by the master or mistress (what was called 'simultaneous instruction', to distinguish it from the 'mutual instruction' of the monitorial schools where in effect the children taught each other). To Wilderspin and Stow is also due the introduction of a separate classroom attached to the schoolroom into which smaller groups of children could be taken in turn.

A number of these early nineteenth-century school buildings have survived but they are rarely in use as schools today and all the original furniture and fittings have disappeared. The method of organization and teaching can be reconstructed from the detailed manuals issued by the National and British School Societies and (for infants) those of the Home and Colonial Society. Where the

large schoolrooms have survived they are either used as an assembly
hall or have been divided up into classrooms.

Much more numerous, and frequently still in use today, are the
two-room schools (i.e. schoolroom with adjoining classroom) which
were the type recommended by the Committee of Council on Education after 1851 (see the Memorandum printed in the Committee's
Minutes, 1851-2, pp. 78-91). School promoters who wished to claim
a Government building grant normally had to comply with the
details laid down in this Memorandum which were subsequently
embodied in a list of *Rules to be observed in planning and fitting-up
schools*, issued in 1863 and at intervals until the end of the nineteenth century. These Rules were the predecessors of the present-day
School Building Regulations.

Essentially, this type of plan, as shown in Fig. 1, consisted of an
oblong schoolroom with three rows of desks arranged along one side
of the room, and with each class separated from the next by a
curtain. These classes were taken by pupil-teachers and, when the
master or mistress wished to address the whole school, the curtains

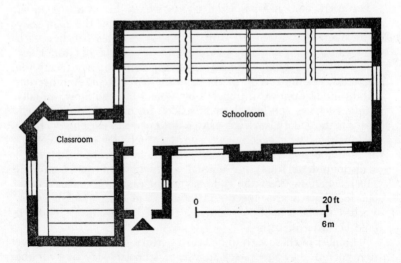

Figure 1   Plan of school showing layout suggested in 1851 by the
Committee of Council on Education. This building was to accommodate seventy-two children in four classes, and variations on this plan
were widely adopted in the second half of the nineteenth century.

would be pulled back to the wall. In the adjoining classroom it was usual to provide a gallery for the infants or for the use of the classes in the main schoolroom who went to the gallery a class at a time. On these occasions the master or mistress gave a 'gallery lesson' using the method of 'simultaneous instruction' or what today we would call 'chalk-and-talk'. In the class divisions of the main schoolroom the pupil-teachers seem mainly to have used a combination of the old monitorial system and oral teaching with the aid of a blackboard. This layout, which was extremely common during the second half of the nineteenth century, was the one originally adopted in the building which is the subject of our first case-study, a small rural school whose building has not been altered because the school population in the area has declined.

A small rural school

This school was erected in 1852 and consists of a large room measuring 36 by 18 feet, with a smaller room 17 by 10 feet leading from it. The large room was designed as the main schoolroom for eighty children, which allowed them 8 square feet each (a standard which was by this date beginning to be accepted as a desirable minimum). The smaller room originally contained the infants' gallery, which has now been removed, as have the long desks in the main room. A former pupil who was at the school in the 1870s, however, recorded the original appearance of the building as follows:

> It was, we believed, a long way ahead of the neighbouring schools, both in construction and position, and had a splendid playground and plenty of nice trees around and great space for games. The desks in the principal room were arranged in three main rows, with divisions made by the drawing of eight-foot-deep red curtains hung on iron brackets and reaching the full depth of the class.... The infants' school lay through a door at the south side, and the seating was provided by a tier of wooden benches like solid boxes on which you could kick your heels and make a good hubbub. The top bench of the tier had the advantage of a good look-out of the window. This room also served for the girls' sewing, knitting, and mending class, one afternoon a week.

What is this school like now, more than a century since it was built? There are only fifteen children on the roll aged from five to eleven and taught by one mistress in the main room. The smaller room is now used only for dining, the meals arriving in containers from a larger school some distance away. About half the area of the large room is occupied by locker desks, which are arranged in three groups for the five to six, seven to eight and nine to ten-year-old children. At the 'infants' end' the desks are butted together to form one working area, but the rest of the desks are in two short rows and at the 'junior end' there is a free-standing blackboard. In the other half of the room are a piano, a sand-tray and smaller music and P.E. equipment. The mistress says that, though she occasionally gives a formal lesson to the older children, most of the teaching is on an individual basis so that she must walk 'thousands of miles' in a year, moving round from one group to the next. The school is in a good decorative state and has a new floor. The high, timbered roof gives the room character but makes it more difficult to heat, though apparently the stove works efficiently. The room is adequately lit in the half of the room where the desks are placed but the other end is rather gloomy owing to lack of windows. There is sufficient wall space for display but there is no sink, so that water for art and craft work has to be fetched from outside. Although there is no hall as such, music, dancing and indoor games can be taken by moving the desks to one end of the room. The only difficulties mentioned by the teacher were the lack of internal toilets and of a fence around the school, which is built on the village green and has in the past suffered minor damage caused by youths in the evening.

Log books of village schools of this type often show that in Victorian and Edwardian times the physical conditions were very poor – the buildings were frequently cold, damp, poorly-ventilated and so on. The condition of such schools today depends very much on whether main services have been brought to the village and on the amount of attention given to the building by the L.E.A., which in an aided school maintains the interior, and by the Managers, who maintain the exterior. Although it is difficult to generalize, conditions seem to have improved considerably since the Second World War, mainly through the carrying out of what are called 'minor' and 'mini-minor' works, i.e. improvements financed with relatively small amounts of money allocated to L.E.A.s by the Department of Education and Science over and above what is allowed for the major building programme. (For what can be done in this way, see the booklet, *The Condition of the Primary Schools in the East Riding of York-shire*, County Hall, Beverley, 1967.) The main administrative objection to small schools of this type is that they are expensive to maintain and make for an uneconomic use of scarce teaching resources. As we shall see later in this book, however, much of value about internal school organization has been learnt from the more individual methods of teaching and the more informal arrangements possible in a small village school of the kind here described.

A school in an industrialized village

Let us now consider a country school which began in 1873 with a building of very similar plan to that described above, but which has been extended at intervals (see Fig. 2) because the village has continued to grow owing to the building of factories in the area. The schoolroom has become two classrooms holding thirty-two children each and the original classroom is now a staffroom and secretary's room combined. The open fireplaces have been replaced with hot-water radiators and some of the Gothic windows have been enlarged.

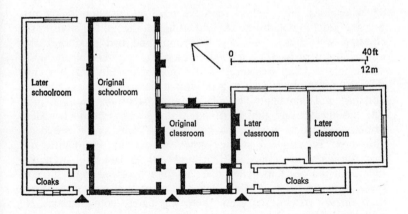

Figure 2 School of 1873, showing original schoolroom and classroom, with later extensions.

The number of children on the roll has increased from 148 in 1873 to 188 now, but the accommodation has been trebled over the last hundred years. As Fig. 2 shows, another large room was subsequently built alongside the original schoolroom and two further classrooms alongside the original classroom. In addition, one class of children is now accommodated in a separate room on an adjoining site; use is also made of the Village Hall for physical education, the Band Hall for school dinners and the public playing fields for games. In 1965 the outside toilets were replaced by a new toilet block immediately adjoining the main school building and in 1966 a new headmaster was appointed who pressed for other improvements in the building, which have been carried out as listed below:

1. The open roofs have been ceiled over, which has improved both the heating and acoustics.
2. Additional display-boards have been put on the walls.
3. The school has been rewired and the lights replaced.
4. Power points have been installed for the use of tape-recorders, record-players and projectors.
5. Some of the floors have been renewed.
6. The old iron desks have been replaced by modern wooden desks for the older children and tables for the infants.
7. Sinks have been installed in three of the classrooms.
8. The whole building has been redecorated.

These changes have helped to make possible the adoption of progressive teaching methods. At the time of the author's visit, the children were busily working in groups and had produced some outstandingly good work, much of which was displayed on the walls. The whole building was cheerful and thoroughly 'alive'. It was clear that the L.E.A. had spent a good deal of money on improving the building, and the supply of books and equipment was also generous. The headmaster said that in his view the essential need in modern primary education was to provide what he called an 'enriched environment' for children as they grow and develop. He pointed out that the adoption of modern teaching methods had only been possible by using every available space in the school and every piece of spare accommodation in the village: even with classes of not more than thirty-two children each, there was barely enough room. He explained that, in order to provide the enriched environment necessary, open areas were needed where children could spread out their work and use educational equipment. A large central space was also needed for P.E., drama, music and movement etc., but there was no hall in the school and the playground could only be used in fine weather. Though classes were kept as small as possible, too much room was taken up by desks, which the headmaster thought were in some respects as inflexible in use as the old cast-iron desks since they took up just as much room and were really suitable only for writing and small-scale activities. More space was needed for the special equipment used in modern mathematics and also for science, wood-work, pottery and other practical activities. Reading was best done in comfortable chairs or lying on a carpeted floor.

The headmaster concluded that the great disadvantage of an old school of this type was that one could not escape from the small classroom units. The box-pattern also prevented the free movement of children from one part of the school to another, while the use of rooms away from the site inhibited movement to the main school, especially in wet weather. While he was appreciative of what had been done to improve the building, he considered that the school had reached the limit of its development and that, since the local school population was still increasing, a new school building had become an urgent necessity.

A school in a redevelopment area

In spite of the limitations of the building occupied by the semi-rural school described above, a great deal of interesting work is clearly taking place there. Much of this is due to a lively headmaster and a team of teachers who work well together, and much to a co-opera-tive L.E.A. which is prepared to spend money on the building and on modern furniture and equipment. In certain districts in some of the major towns, however, serious social problems have arisen and schools in slum-clearance areas have all too often been allowed to run down with the housing among which they are situated. The contrast between the rationale of such schools when they were first used and their present state can be instructive.

Our example this time is a Church school erected in 1876, the plan of which is shown in Fig. 3. The ground floor was originally occupied by the infant department (or school as it was called then) and consisted of a long, narrow schoolroom with two classrooms leading off it and a somewhat larger classroom, added in 1880, to one side. The dimensions and accommodation of the infant school

as originally provided (at 8 square feet per pupil) are set out in the
school log book as follows:

Room	Length × breadth	Area	Accommodation
Schoolroom	65 × 20 ft.	1,300 sq. ft.	$162\frac{1}{2}$
Classroom 1	20 × 16 ft.	320 sq. ft.	40
Classroom 2	20 × 16 ft.	320 sq. ft.	40
Classroom 3	30 × 18 ft.	540 sq. ft.	$67\frac{1}{2}$
Total number of pupils to be accommodated			310

The original plans of the school do not show the furniture layout
but there was certainly a raised gallery in the main infant schoolroom, as was usual at this period, since the sides of what is now the
hall show where it once stood: there is similar evidence of galleries

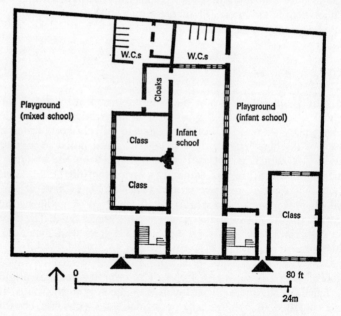

Figure 3 Church school, built 1876–80. The first-floor plan was
identical.

in some of the classrooms. The mixed school (i.e. for children between seven and twelve and above) occupied the first floor, which
consisted of a schoolroom and three classrooms of the same dimensions as in the infant school and with the same accommodation
figure of 310 children.

The log books show that the number of children in attendance
varied a good deal during the Victorian period – chiefly owing to
epidemics during the winter months. The number on the roll dropped
when Board schools were opened nearby, but increased when fees
were virtually abolished after 1891. Many of the children in the
infant school were under five years of age and were taught in a
'babies' class'; some seven-year-old children were also taught as
Standard I in the infant school before moving upstairs to the mixed
school. The babies' class and Standard I were in separate classrooms,
the rest of the infants occupying the third classroom and the principal schoolroom. The total numbers rarely rose above 600, but, when
they did, conditions became extremely difficult, especially if a member of staff fell ill (the normal staffing provision in each school was
a certificated teacher as head, with two adult but uncertificated assistant teachers, and two pupil-teachers). It is clear that classes were
often extremely large (in the sixty to seventy range) and all the
teachers, particularly the pupil-teachers, who would themselves have
been only in their 'teens, were very hard pressed. The job of the two
head teachers was to check on the work of all the classes in turn and
to take over any class for a particular subject or during the absence
of the normal teacher. In the mixed school on the first floor very
great importance was attached to preparing the children to pass the
Standards which were laid down by the government and examined by
an H.M. Inspector once a year.

The references in the log books to the building and internal organization are relatively few. The rigidity of the teaching methods employed is, however, indicated by the H.M.I.'s report on the school
in 1878:

The Infants have been carefully and successfully drilled in
reading, writing, counting and marching. The object lessons
seem to have been too mechanical. No lines of poetry have
been committed to memory. This serious omission should be
remedied forthwith.
   In the Mixed School the children have been carefully
taught and on the whole with satisfactory results. A
few upright shafts in each room would greatly improve the

ventilation in weather too cold to allow the windows
to be opened.

Significant changes occurred in the 1890s as a direct result of new
developments in teaching methods and curriculum. Cookery and
dressmaking were taught more systematically to the senior girls,
who went to an adjoining centre provided by the School Board. Draw-
ing was introduced for the boys and Swedish drill, presumably taken
in the small playground, was begun in 1895. In the infant school one
can trace a distinct change of methods deriving essentially from
Froebelian ideas, which were at last beginning to penetrate into the
ordinary elementary schools. In 1891 a new headmistress introduced
cube-building, stick-laying and mat-plaiting, which were among the
so-called 'kindergarten occupations'. The headmistress also told the
teachers that the lessons would be far pleasanter for both teachers and
scholars 'if the former would chat more to the children and thus
encourage them to give out more freely their own little ideas'. Marching began to receive special attention and provision was made 'for the
babies either to march round the principal room or the largest
classroom, as their own room affords such poor scope for the practice of this valuable exercise'.

By the 1890s, therefore, this school building was beginning to become inadequate for what were then new educational developments.
What is the situation today? The building can now only be made to
work at all by a drastic reduction of numbers – from a maximum of
620 when the school was first built to the present 221, organized as
an eight-class junior school for boys and girls. The structural altera-
tions made since 1880 have been very few, since any extension (or
even the erection of temporary classrooms in the playground) is quite
impossible owing to the very restricted site, which fronts the road and
is surrounded on its three other sides by houses. Of the four very small
classrooms, one is now used as a staffroom and one as a television
room; the other two house only twenty-five children each. What
was originally the infant schoolroom has been divided into two by a
brick wall to make a classroom of reasonable size on one side and a
seriously undersized hall (which is also used for dining) on the other.
On the first floor, what was the main schoolroom of the mixed school
has been divided up into three classrooms by glazed partitions, which
in theory can be moved but in practice rarely are. The open fireplaces have been blocked up and replaced by high-level gas fires, and
fluorescent strip-lighting has been installed; paper towels have replaced the roller towels used until recently, but the toilets are still in

a congested corner of the playground.

The general impression of the building remains one of squalor and neglect. Although the staff are making brave efforts to overcome the difficulties imposed by the building and by the area generally, this is a clear case of the architecture of a school severely restricting the kind of teaching and learning which can be carried on. The deficiencies of the building must also add considerably to the social problems posed by the area as a whole.

Another urban school

Since about half of the primary school buildings in use are of nine-teenth-century origin, it is worth giving one more example of the kind of difficulties faced by teachers in at least some of these schools today. Thus we may take an urban school of 1872 now used entirely by infant children. In the summer of 1970 there were 196 children in five classes, one of which has to be accommodated in the hall, which is also used for dining. The headmistress makes the following points about her building:

1. The hall is now used as a fifth classroom thus cutting down its use for dramatic play, music, movement and P.E. (in poor weather). Using the hall for school dinners also means that the class in the hall has to move painting-easels, models, or other craft work from the main part of the hall so that dinner tables can be set out. The hall faces a busy main road on one side, so that it is impossible to have one set of windows open because of traffic noise. At other times in the day it is impossible to have the opposite set of windows open because of the noise from the pupils in the adjoining junior school, who have their playtime at a different time to the infants.

2. Since the classrooms are small, the corridor is often used by the children for painting, dramatic work and measuring. Had the corri-dor been twice as wide when originally built there would be adequate space to use it as a classroom annexe and as a passageway between the classes and the hall. The corridor at one end has to be permanently lit by electric light. Glass tiles in the roof have been re-quested, but as yet to no avail.

3. The classrooms are too small for forty children and it is some-times necessary, for example, to move a child in order to get at a cupboard. In addition, the classrooms have no outlet into the play-ground. This makes it difficult for teachers to encourage group work outside, since they are not readily available to assist children when

they need help. Classrooms two, three and four have glass and wooden partitions which, if opened up, would prove useful in team-teaching situations, allowing more integration between the classes and giving more space. (This situation is under review at the moment, but staff are loath to share their own four walls with others as yet.)

4. The cloakrooms are at either end of the school, positioned quite well for easy access into the school, but not large enough to hold nearly 200 coats, slipper-bags, hats, gloves and wellington boots.

5. The lavatories are across the playground, but in bad weather children have indoor basement ones for their use. These latter have the disadvantage of accommodating twelve children only and are reached by two flights of steps.

6. All entrances to the school have five steps. This makes it difficult for children and teachers to take apparatus into the playground for P.E. or other activities.

7. The windows throughout the school are too high for children to look out. Interesting things going on outside the classrooms can only be noted when the children are in the playground and the first fall of snow has to be noted from a chair-standing position.

8. The only available space to house a library is in one of the entrances into school. This has been used for two terms now as a library, with a carpet bought from school funds. Its disadvantages are two-fold since (a) the door to the basement toilets is at this entrance and (b) visitors to the school constantly use the entrance although there is a notice asking them not to.

9. In the basement there is a store-cupboard and a good-sized room for furniture storage. It is hoped to use the latter as a craftroom with whitewashed walls for the children to paint on, but at present it is too damp and dimly-lit.

10. The playground also presents teaching problems. It is shared with nearly 400 juniors so that one cannot use the playground at will – so necessary with infants who may want to explore something outside but cannot do so because of junior P.E.

11. One would conclude from the above points that teaching in this school is constantly fraught with frustrations. This is not so, but the teaching is affected by lack of space, limitations on the use of the playground, the position of the hall in relation to the classrooms and the rigid timetable which has to be adhered to in order to enable everyone to use the hall at some time.

3 The central-hall plan

The introduction of class teaching

We noticed in the last chapter that new teaching methods were being introduced into the elementary schools in the 1890s, with kindergarten activities in the infant departments and more practical work in the senior departments. Two other major changes took place towards the end of the nineteenth century and the beginning of the twentieth which also had important effects on the planning and architecture of schools.

The first arose from the sheer size of the problem of universal compulsory education. The Elementary Education Act of 1870 set up school boards and permitted them to make attendance at school compulsory between the ages of five and thirteen. But it was not until 1880 that compulsion was universally introduced up to the age of ten and the problems of securing full attendance remained considerable until fees were abolished in the majority of elementary schools in 1891. The minimum leaving age was raised to eleven in 1893 and to twelve six years later and an increasing number of children remained on voluntarily at school beyond the minimum leaving age, a tendency which continued into the early twentieth century. The result was that large classes became normal and the need to design very large school buildings to accommodate them became pressing.

Secondly, the staffing of elementary schools was undergoing a major change. In 1895, out of a total teaching staff in England and Wales of 112,000, less than half (53,000) were certificated, the balance being made up with 28,000 uncertificated assistant teachers and 31,000 pupil-teachers. The pupil-teachers were young people (mainly female) aged between fourteen and eighteen and they needed careful supervision by the head teacher. The existence of this large body of trainee-teachers at first tended to encourage the perpetuation of the traditional one-schoolroom plan, for in a room like that shown in Fig. 1 it was easier for the head teacher to keep a close eye on the pupil-teachers taking their classes in different parts of the room.

Early in the twentieth century, however, important changes took place in the whole system of teacher-training. It was decided that pupil-teachers should be largely replaced by student-teachers recruited not from the elementary schools at the age of fourteen but from the secondary schools at sixteen, after which they should do part-time teaching in the elementary schools until eighteen before going on to training colleges. Although the number of unqualified assistant teachers remained large, the virtual disappearance of the

pupil-teachers early in the twentieth century meant that elementary school staff could be given more responsibility and could safely be
left to teach classes accommodated in separate rooms.

Origin of the central-hall plan

The need for very large schools had been tackled by the major school
boards soon after they had been set up in 1870. The London School
Board, in particular, was faced with enormous problems arising from
the size of its child population, and the Architect to the Board,
E. R. Robson, gave systematic attention to the whole question of
school building in his book, *School Architecture*, first published in
1874. He pointed out that previous architectural experience had
mainly been of building relatively small Church schools and he
stressed the need to build in a new civic style and on a much larger
scale than ever before. The various plans devised by the London
School Board during the thirty years of its existence are clearly
summarized in T. A. Spalding's *The Work of the London School
Board*, 1900, ch. 3, and Felix Clay's *Modern School Buildings*, 1902,
pp. 308-11. The main tendency was to increase the number of classrooms along the sides of a central corridor, which gradually widened
to become a hall used for general assemblies and for teaching two or
more of the classes. This in turn developed into the so-called 'central-
hall plan' with classrooms leading off the hall on three or four sides,
a plan which was also adopted by many of the other large school
boards (e.g. as early as 1878 the Birmingham School Board began to
adopt the 'Prussian system' as it was also called because the elementary schools of Prussia, which were regarded as models in their day,
were organized on the basis of separate classrooms for each class).

The central-hall plan was therefore associated with the building of
very large schools and also reflected the greater degree of confidence
which was being placed in the assistant teachers, who were now
thought to be capable of taking classes physically isolated from each
other. It was, however, usual for the walls separating the classrooms
from the hall to be partially glazed so that the head of the school
could still see how the children were behaving. In most schools of
this type which are still in use the glazed partitions have been covered
with large sheets of paper by the teachers, whose desire for privacy
has grown ever greater since about 1900.

This type of plan gradually spread throughout the country, and
to infant schools as well as those for older children. It was claimed that

classes of up to sixty children could easily be controlled in such schools, where it was usual to have a stepped floor so that the teacher could more easily see the children at the back of the class. The Lancasterian schools had earlier had a sloping floor for the same reason and a stepped floor was also used in some schools in the middle of the nineteenth century, but the floor remained level for most later schools. Then in the late nineteenth and early twentieth centuries, when larger numbers of children had to be controlled by a single teacher, the stepped floor often reappeared. Another change which went on at about the same time was the gradual replacement of the pupils' long desks by dual desks which made it easier for the teachers to pass between the rows and exercise firmer discipline over the children. (See J. H. Cowham's *School Organization, Hygiene, Discipline and Ethics*, 1899, pp. 148-9, for a contemporary discussion of the pros and cons of benches and desks.) In the infant schools, galleries had been common since the early nineteenth century and were still in use at the end of it. The introduction of the stepped floor into schools of all types was tending, however, to make the traditional gallery less necessary and the importance which was just

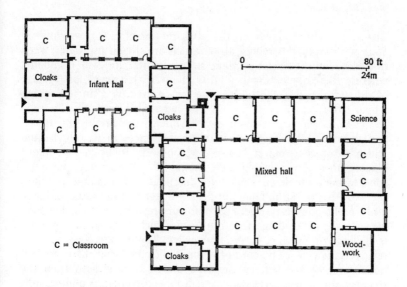

Figure 4   Infant and junior schools, built 1894-9

beginning to be attached to freer movement for very young children led to their gradual disappearance in the inter-war period.

A large number of schools were built on the central-hall plan up to the First World War and many are still in use. What are they like to teach in now? In order to answer this question, let us take two schools built as Board schools on the same site and which are still in use today (see plan, Fig. 4). The first was built as an infant school for children under seven years of age and including, as in many other places, far more children below the age of five than became usual later. The second was the mixed school for children between seven and twelve or more (remembering that there was an increasing number of children staying on beyond the minimum leaving age, so that by the First World War a clear distinction was coming to be made in many elementary schools between the 'junior' and 'senior' sections of the school). The infant school was single-storey but the mixed school two storeys in height. In other places it was more usual to have a three-storey building, with infants on the ground floor, girls on the second and boys on the third floor – all with basically the same layout.

The infant school

The infant school (shown on the left-hand side of Fig. 4) was built in 1894 with eight classrooms, all of which are still in use. They were, however, built to accommodate sixty children in each originally, whereas there are now 240 infants in seven classrooms (an average of thirty-four), the eighth classroom being used by a nursery group which has recently been started. The log book records that in 1899 the H.M.I. reported briefly that 'the infants are bright and happy and they are well taught'. There are references to the curriculum which show that 'object lessons', which were traditional in infant schools, formed the staple diet, though these seemed to have become rather more detailed in content including, for example, not only the usual horse, cat and dog but 'legs and feet of birds, beaks of birds, birds' nests, migratory birds, and birds of prey'. In 1900 the log book gives details of 'kindergarten occupations' such as mat-weaving, clay-modelling, ring-laying, thread-laying, etc. These were, as we saw, a relatively new development but it should be noted that these 'occupations' were of a sedentary character and it is clear both from the recollections of retired teachers and from contemporary photographs of infant schools that the teaching remained formal, with the children still sitting at their desks. One retired infants' headmistress recalled that the 'gift boxes', which were part of the Froebel apparatus, were opened by the children at a word of command, the exact opposite of what Froebel had intended.

The only structural change made in the infant school building since it was first erected is the recent addition of a staffroom near the main entrance to the school. The stepped floors in the classrooms have been levelled and sinks have been installed in some of the classrooms. The furniture has been renewed, including tables of modern design for some of the classes and plastic trays for the children's belongings, which are stored on wall-shelves when not in use. There is space to do this only because the classrooms now accommodate many fewer children than they were originally designed for and, even so, several of the classrooms now seem very congested. Storage of material has become a problem because far more of it is used than when the school was built. In one classroom, for example, a group of children had made a large model castle out of cardboard boxes and cones but there was no space to display it. In another classroom the teacher and children were showing signs of discomfort because of the direct sunlight which entered the room. Venetian blinds had been lowered but the windows had been kept closed since, according to the teacher, the blinds rattled excessively when the windows were opened and the top windows in any case could not be opened because the blinds were in the way. (It should be added that cross-ventilation was impossible because of the design of the building.)

The headmistress of this infant school, who has recently been appointed, had some interesting comments about the design of the school in the light of modern teaching methods. She had no wish to force an 'integrated day' or 'team-teaching'[1] on to the staff since she said that they were far too wedded at present to the idea of taking their own classes in their own rooms. The hall was already used by the classes in turn for P.E., music, movement and so on, but she would like to see it used more as a central resource area. Since in her view the classrooms were not big enough for the children to carry on all the various activities needed in a modern infant school, she was beginning to set up 'activity corners' in various parts of the hall which could be used by groups of children from any of the classes as the need arose. Already there was a 'library corner' and she was planning a 'music corner' for home-made instruments and as a place where two

[1] For detailed definitions of these and other terms in current use, see the glossaries in *Children and their Primary Schools*, I, 537-41, and S. C. Mason, *In our Experience*, 188-90. See also p. 62 below.

or three children could practise. One teacher with whom the head-mistress discussed this idea said that she thought it was an excellent plan, so long as the music corner was not outside her room ! But one of the other teachers, who was keen on music, said that she was look-ing forward to taking responsibility for the equipment when it was placed adjoining her room. The headmistress, as in most of the infant schools visited, had already established good relationships with the staff and new ideas were freely discussed among them (mainly in the staffroom, which was also used by the head though she had her own room too).

The headmistress did not think that the children in the various activity corners would be unduly distracted by the other more general activities going on in the hall. Nor did she think that noise from the hall interfered with the work going on in the classrooms. The question of noise can be a problem in any school of central-hall type, but, as the headmistress pointed out, much depends on the type of teaching going on in the school. The teachers were not 'giving lec-tures' to their classes, which would require completely quiet con-ditions: they were carrying on 'personal conversations' with indi-viduals and small groups, and both teachers and children readily accepted a reasonable level of 'purposeful noise'.

The mixed school

The original mixed school (shown on the right of Fig. 4) was built in 1899 for over 1,000 children accommodated in fourteen classrooms on the ground floor and four on the first floor, based on an allowance of 10 square feet per child. Originally, two pairs of classrooms were divi-ded by sliding partitions and two classes were also taught in the hall. The design of the school reflected the curricular changes which were taking place at the turn of the nineteenth century because two of the rooms on the ground floor were intended for science and wood-work and an upstairs room for cookery.

The structural changes which have taken place since 1899 have again been relatively few. The original practical rooms are now ordinary classrooms, all the classroom floors have been levelled and the hall floor renewed. Fluorescent lighting has been installed and modern hot-water radiators have replaced the original heating sys-tem. Wash-basins have been installed in some classrooms. The school was substantially built and the possibilities of changing the basic classroom pattern are therefore very limited.

This school has, however, the considerable advantage that it now has to cater for only 340 children, all of junior age. The classrooms have remained the same size (about 600 square feet) but they now each accommodate only an average of thirty-five children, compared with the sixty for which they were originally designed. There are also a number of spare classrooms which are now used for other educational purposes. Thus one classroom is used for showing T.V. programmes, two others are used for dining (and as a youth centre in the evenings) and two others for remedial reading and as a central book-store. The original design included a staffroom, which, though small by present-day standards, is still usable. The headmaster and secretary also have their own rooms.

Because of the relatively small number of children and the improvements carried out by the L.E.A. in lighting, heating and so on, this school, in spite of its somewhat forbidding exterior, may be said to have adapted well to modern conditions. The number of children on the roll is, however, expected to increase, which will mean using the T.V. room as an ordinary classroom. In addition, the two classrooms now used for dining are very unattractive and the youth club which uses it in the evenings had left chewing gum on the floor and marks on the pictures hanging on the walls. The headmaster liked the central hall which, he said, acted as a focal point – he often stands there himself and can talk to teachers and children as they move about the school. The hall is used for morning assembly, P.E., drama, dancing and singing. The acoustics in the hall are not good, however, since the high ceiling produces an echo. The head did not think that the noise of the various activities going on in the hall disturbed the adjoining classes because the classroom walls, though glazed, were fairly solid.

The headmaster pointed out that the school was sited in the middle of 'a brick and concrete jungle', i.e. it is completely surrounded by Victorian and Edwardian housing. He would like to have more grass and trees but he added that at least the school was part of the local community and there was a large park not far away into which the children could go for nature study. What he would mainly like would be a new dining hall and also a covered space outside for P.E. because he could then make more use of the hall for other activities.

How far was the generally optimistic picture given by the headmaster borne out by the views of the class teachers? In one classroom an experienced male member of staff was taking a fourth-year class, which at the time of the visit consisted of thirty-eight children sitting in groups of dual locker desks and working out arithmetical problems. The room was slightly congested and the teacher thought that with more than thirty-five children the classroom was really too small, especially when art and craft activities were taking place. He would like to 'overflow' into the hall (with modelling work for example) but this was not possible because of the other activities taking place there. The noise from the hall was not excessive but some classrooms were more affected than others in this respect. The acoustics in his classroom were not good – if a child moved and scraped the chair-leg 'a word was lost'. The heating was good but the ventilation was poor : the top windows were difficult to open and if the bottom windows were opened they let in dust from the road. The windows (the bottom sill of which, as in the other classrooms, was about 5 feet from the floor) were too high and tended to make the room gloomy and to give a 'closed-in effect'. There were storage cupboards, which were adequate but not easy for the children to use, and the blackboard was very old and needed replacing. The use of visual aids was difficult because the electricity point was of an old-fashioned type and the blackout blinds did not work : in addition, the children at the front of the class were too near the screen and those on the edges of the class could not see the screen properly. He thought that the main advantage of the central-hall plan was the sense of community it fostered. Certainly he preferred this plan to that of the previous school he had worked in, which was of post-war design and which he recalled chiefly for its long corridors and icy blasts of air.

Other criticisms of the central-hall plan

Schools of this pattern continued to be built in large numbers up to the First World War. The schools just considered are fortunate in having much smaller numbers of children to teach than those for which they were originally designed. In places where the school population has continued to rise the difficulties are naturally greater and we may take as an example a school built in 1913 on the central-hall plan which is now used by both infants and juniors, and where the large number of children has obliged the L.E.A. to erect no less than six hutted classrooms in various parts of the playground. Here is a list of points made by a relatively young woman teacher in this school :

    1. The shared hall restricts the number of practical periods, and

when assemblies etc. are going on people are marooned inside their rooms.

2. In bad weather classes coming to use the hall have to wear coats and boots and there is no suitable place to keep them.

3. In the main building there is no water-supply in the classrooms.

4. The rooms in the main building are so small that children must sit in rows and be formally taught. Any thought of groups or moving is impossible.

5. The school is so scattered that children and staff often do not see each other for weeks. The staff cannot get to the staffroom for breaks and therefore the interchange of ideas is difficult.

6. The numerous 'ins and outs' around the huts make the yard difficult to supervise.

7. In the huts the heating is inefficient and the hollowness under the floor magnifies noise from feet. They are also acoustically poor.

8. Playground space is decreasing whilst numbers are increasing, so that the local park must be used for games because all the children cannot get into the yard.

9. There is no spare space where children can get away from the class for private activity.

10. The building is inflexible so that one has to think in units of classes.

Many of the disadvantages listed above arise from conditions of overcrowding which would make teaching difficult whatever the original design of the building, but some are intrinsic to the central-hall plan. This plan, as we saw earlier, was essentially designed for classroom teaching and it may be said that the more teachers are trying to get away from teaching the class as a unit of thirty to forty children, the more likely they are to be dissatisfied with such a plan. Much depends on the size of the original classrooms, bearing in mind the loss of space with radiator pipes and the type of furniture in use. In some schools of this kind the classrooms are smaller than in later schools which makes it harder to divide the children into groups, since desks arranged informally tend to take up more room than if set out in rows. The greatest limitation of the central-hall plan, however, is that when the hall is being used by a class for dancing, P.E., etc., the other classes have to be confined to their rooms, which can mean for most of the time.

Some changes are clearly possible, however, where the numbers are not too large. We saw in the infant school of 1894 discussed above that the headmistress was beginning to use the hall as a resource centre, i.e. as a place where children from any class could go. The main justification for such a change was stated to be that it was more convenient to have specialized equipment in specialized areas and to make the most of the particular interests of the staff by giving them certain activities to supervise. A similar tendency was discernible in the junior school of 1899, in that certain rooms had been given specialized functions (remedial reading and T.V.). Inside the classrooms, both in the infant and junior schools, children worked in groups, though there were occasions when the teacher addressed the whole class at once. Working in groups was explained as being more 'natural' and 'sociable' and some references were also made to the varied abilities of the children, which suggested that in some cases the classes were divided into groups according to the children's ability, particularly in mathematics and reading. As in the earlier schools considered, one notices the marked tendency in many primary schools today to occupy every available space for use by groups of children, often working by themselves. Some of the rambling old schools, however, seem to provide more opportunity for this than the more rigid plans of the central-hall type, and of the quadrangular type which we now go on to consider.

4 Veranda and quadrangle plans

The welfare state and its influence

The central-hall plan dominated school architecture, as we have seen, until the outbreak of the First World War. During the inter-war period, however, a number of developments took place which radically altered the design of new primary schools. These architectural developments were themselves intimately bound up with contemporary changes in educational ideas and practices and in society as a whole.

So far as the size of schools was concerned, the achievement of universal compulsory education by the end of the nineteenth century, taken with the declining birthrate after about 1900, meant that less stress was placed on building very large schools. The number of children staying on voluntarily at school beyond the statutory minimum leaving age of twelve was counter-balanced by a sharp decline in the number of children under the age of five attending the ordinary elementary schools. Early in the twentieth century educationists interested in the teaching of very young children criticized the mechanical way in which Froebelian methods were being practised in the infant schools (the 'occupations' to which reference was made in the last chapter) and advocated the setting up of 'free kindergartens', or nursery schools as they were more generally known after 1918. Unfortunately, the decline in the number of children under five years old attending ordinary infant schools was not made up by a corresponding increase in separate nursery schools, and the percentage of the three to five age-group in elementary schools dropped from forty-three in 1900 to fifteen by 1920. (For a full discussion of these developments, see the report of the Consultative Committee, *Infant and Nursery Schools*, 1933, ch. 1, especially the table on p. 29.)

Another important factor which affected school design was that the pattern of urban development after about 1900 was such that new schools came to be built on the peripheries of the towns, where more spacious sites were available. This tendency was accentuated in the inter-war period when many families from slum areas in the urban centres were rehoused on new housing estates on the edges of the towns, or in the open countryside outside them. In architectural terms this had the result of increasing the number of single-storey elementary schools, with a corresponding enlargement of school sites.

The rehousing of families from slum areas was only one expression of the greater concern that was now being shown for the health and physical well-being of the poorer classes in the community. The official provision of school meals and medical inspection of children which began in the first decade of the twentieth century was an equally important reflection of the new 'welfare' policy pursued by central and local government authorities. Characteristically, one of the main objections which was beginning to be made to the central-hall plan was its alleged deficiencies in providing proper lighting and ventilation. In a school designed on the central-hall pattern only one side of each classroom is normally in contact with the outside air: one side adjoins the hall, and there are usually other classrooms on each of the other two sides. With this arrangement, therefore, cross-ventilation is impossible and it was this deficiency which doctors began to stress just at the time when medical inspection was being introduced and open-air schools were being advocated for delicate and tubercular children.

The veranda school

It was this desire to secure cross-ventilation which led to the building of so-called veranda schools, a development which was pioneered by the school architects of Staffordshire and Derbyshire shortly before the First World War and widely adopted thereafter. (For details of the early Derbyshire schools see P. A. Robson, *School-Planning*, 1911, especially pp. 55-7.) The new and at that time revolutionary principle adopted was to detach the classrooms from the hall. The classrooms could then be arranged in rows, with glazed folding doors instead of side walls, so that during the summer months these doors could be opened out and a free flow of fresh air secured. Open verandas were also provided to give access to the classrooms and shelter from wind and rain when the doors were open. In the winter months a flow of air across the room was ensured by providing high-level clerestory windows above the verandas. (For an interesting discussion of the whole question of school ventilation see F. Clay's *Modern School Buildings*, 1929, ch. 3.)

Schools of this type consciously imitated the open-air schools for delicate children which were also being built at this time. By the 1920s, however, the plan had been slightly modified by providing folding doors and a veranda on only one side of the classroom block (usually the more sheltered side and frequently opening on to a quadrangle or grassed courtyard). The essential principle of cross-ventilated classrooms had, however, so far become the accepted orthodoxy of school-planning that the report of the Consultative Committee, *The Primary School*, 1931, p. xvii, categorically stated that 'The more closely the design of the primary school approaches that of the open-air school the better'; and the Board of Education in its pamphlet on *Elementary School Buildings*, 1936, p. 12, advised architects that 'The ideal should be envisaged as a single-storey building, opened out to the air and sunshine in every part'.

New educational ideas

Before we look in more detail at some of the schools built on this plan during the inter-war period, we need to consider other changes which were leading to modifications in the curricula and internal organization of the elementary schools. For a detailed exposition the reader is referred to R. D. Bramwell's *Elementary School Work 1900–1925* (1961) and to G. A. N. Lowndes's *The Silent Social Revolution* (1969, chs 7 and 8). Here it will be sufficient to mention some of the major changes which directly affected school architecture and organization. These in fact are hard to pin-point because there was a general change in attitude towards children which affected different people at different times: we know when leading educational theorists began to expound their ideas, but their influence is not easy to trace outside the relatively few schools which made a special point of practising and publicizing them. The American John Dewey published perhaps his most influential book *The School and Society* in 1899 and his ideas of 'child-centred' education were popularized in England in J. J. Findlay's *The Child and the Curriculum* of 1906, with its stress on 'learning by doing' and working through 'projects' rather than 'subjects'. In 1911 Rachel and Margaret McMillan opened their pioneer nursery school at Deptford, and a translation of Dr Maria Montessori's book, *The Montessori Method*, appeared in the following year. The journal *New Era*, which expressed the ideas of the upholders of 'progressive' education, was founded in 1920 and Miss Helen Parkhurst's *Education on the Dalton Plan* was published in 1923.

The ideas of these and other educational writers of the period led to a number of important changes in the attitude of teachers towards children, especially very young children. Greater attention was paid to children's 'natural' interests, and to 'realistic' curricula and 'active' methods of learning. The 1931 report, *The Primary School*, summed up the fundamental change of outlook as follows (p. xvi):

During the last forty years, and with increasing rapidity in
the twelve years since 1918, the outlook of the primary school
has been broadened and humanised. Today it includes care,
through the school medical service, for the physical welfare of
children, offers larger, if still inadequate, opportunities for
practical activity, and handles the curriculum, not only as
consisting of lessons to be mastered, but as providing fields of
new and interesting experience to be explored; it appeals less
to passive obedience and more to the sympathy, social spirit
and imagination of the children, relies less on mass instruction
and more on the encouragement of individual and group work,
and treats the school, in short, not as the antithesis of life, but as
its complement and commentary.

This basic change in outlook must also be considered in relation to
the earlier report of the Consultative Committee, *The Education of
the Adolescent*, 1926, which advocated the setting up of separate
'senior' or 'modern' schools for children over the age of eleven, and
the Committee's later report, *Infant and Nursery Schools*, 1933,
which further developed a distinctive rationale for the education of
primary school children.

How school design was affected

How did these changes in the outlook of educationists influence the
design of schools? The adoption of the veranda-type plan, though
it was accompanied by great improvements in the physical surroundings of schools, did not change the fundamental idea of the class as
the basic unit of organization. Indeed, by separating each classroom
from the next and making the hall structurally distinct from the
classrooms, it could be argued that the new type of plan destroyed
the educational and architectural unity which had characterized
earlier school buildings. It should be noted, however, that the hall
was retained and its importance was in fact particularly emphasized
in the new schools of the 1920s and 1930s partly at least to counter-
act the potentially disruptive effects of dividing the school into
separate classroom units. The hall was seen to be essential for morning assemblies, which encouraged the development of a community
spirit, as well as giving space for physical exercises and musical
activities of the kind which educationists were vigorously advocating
at this period.

While, however, this dispersal of the classrooms was counter-balanced by the greater use of the hall for communal activities, there is no doubt that the 'streaming' of classes in preparation for the 'scholarship examination' to grammar schools led to undue segregation of the classes in some primary schools. Two training college lecturers, Mary Sturt and Ellen Oakden, in their book, *Matter and Method in Education* (1931), were expressing a point of view which was increasingly gaining acceptance during this period when they wrote (p. 248) that 'children of the same mental age are much better fitted to work together in most subjects' and that 'when considering the make-up of a class, it is important to get children with approximately the same I.Q. into the same classes'.

The beginning of group work

While the class remained, on the whole, the basic teaching unit during the inter-war period considerable efforts were made to reduce the size of classes, the L.C.C. leading the way with its policy of limiting infant classes to forty-eight and those for older children to forty. In the 1930s one also notices that the whole concept of class-teaching was beginning to receive critical examination, especially in the infant schools. Essentially, this sprang from the importance attached to individual and group work by the 'progressives' of the previous decade. The two college lecturers quoted above considered that many of the criticisms made of class-teaching had been justified, but 'it is highly doubtful whether the oral lesson can be done away with altogether' (p. 130). A similar balance between teaching the whole class and organizing group and individual work was struck in the 1931 report, *The Primary School* (p. xxiii) which also realized that with the introduction of group activities 'the function of the teacher is less that of an expositor than of an adviser and consultant'.

Some of the new school buildings of the 1930s reflected this greater emphasis on working in small groups. It was usual to provide tables and chairs which could be arranged in groups, rather than locker desks with fixed seats which were too heavy to move easily. The Board of Education's pamphlet, *Elementary School Buildings*, 1936, also mentioned the desirability of having tables and wall lockers instead of locker desks, and further recommended that the standard classroom should be 520 feet square and designed for forty pupils, with some larger rooms for practical activities, not only in senior but junior schools as well.

A study of the plans of schools actually built during the inter-war period, and of contemporary photographs of school interiors, suggests, however, that many of the recommendations about group work and more informal teaching methods remained theoretical, except in the nursery and more progressive infant schools. The usual arrangement in infant and junior schools was to provide classrooms measuring 480 square feet and designed for forty-eight children arranged in four rows of dual desks with aisles between. In senior schools the standard classroom also measured 480 square feet, but it was designed for forty instead of forty-eight children, and larger rooms were also provided for woodwork, domestic science and other practical subjects. An illustrated book entitled *The Schools at Work*, which was issued by the National Union of Teachers in about 1932 and which clearly aimed at illustrating the best of contemporary practice, shows the children in junior schools sitting in formal rows facing the teacher, and only in the pictures of nursery and infant schools are group activities shown. One is bound to conclude that, in spite of all the 'progressive' educational writings of the period, much formal class-teaching continued to take place, though the curriculum was certainly being broadened, especially in the new senior schools.

The quadrangular plan

The building of new housing estates during the inter-war period and the reorganization of elementary education on the lines advocated in the Hadow Report of 1926 encouraged the building of new infant, junior and senior schools. Infant and junior schools were often built on the same site and invariably shared the use of a hall placed between the two schools. Where the schools were for a relatively small number of children the classrooms were arranged in straight rows, but when a large number of classrooms were needed it was usual to build them around quadrangles linked by the shared hall.

A typical quadrangular plan with infant and junior schools sharing the same site is shown in Fig. 5. It will be noted that the veranda principle was maintained but also that, if one compares it with the central-hall plan in Fig. 4, what basically has happened is that the central halls have been replaced by open quadrangles. Access to the classrooms is by way of the verandas, which run round the sides of the quadrangles and originally consisted merely of lean-to roofs supported by iron columns. There are large folding doors which can open the sides of the classrooms to the verandas, above which are high-level windows to provide cross-ventilation when these doors are closed.

An infant school of 1926

Let us first consider the infant school shown on the right-hand side of the plan in Fig. 5. This school was originally planned with six classrooms, four of which were to accommodate forty-eight children and two were for forty-two (a total of 276). The classrooms formed two sides of a quadrangle, the third side being occupied by the hall and the fourth by cloakrooms and rooms for the headmistress and staff. The toilets were placed nearby but (as in earlier schools) they were outside the main building.

Today all the classrooms are still in use by infants but one of the classrooms is used for remedial reading, for which children from

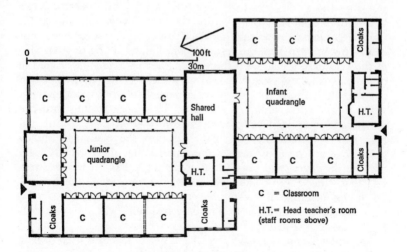

Figure 5 Infant and junior schools, built 1926, with verandas to the classrooms and open quadrangles

various classes are withdrawn for specialist teaching. The remaining five classrooms have between thirty and thirty-five children each, making a total of 161. There are two other classes in the school, which are housed in adjoining wooden huts. The original building therefore accommodates considerably fewer children than it was designed for in 1926. The child population on the estate has declined because the young married couples of the 1920s are now elderly people whose children have in many cases left the estate. In 1928 there were no less than 460 children in the infant school, including a class of fifty which had to be taken in the hall, with other rooms near the school also used for teaching. In this respect, therefore, the pressure has eased, though in another respect changes in social habits have increased the pressure on accommodation. This is because a large proportion of the children now at the school stay for school dinners and, since the hall is used by the junior school for dining, the infants have to use two of the classrooms. A scullery has been built at one end of the hall to serve meals to both the infant and junior schools.

In what other respects has the original design been changed? The headmistress said that both she and her staff appreciated the quadrangle in the centre of the school, which has been grassed over and planted with flowers. However, this was mainly a matter of aesthetics since the garden was used very little for teaching purposes. The headmistress said that the weather was not usually fine enough to use the garden area for children's activities and access to it was not easy. This in turn was the result of the failure of the original idea of the verandas. It had been found that the open verandas made the classrooms cold and draughty and they had recently been closed in (an alteration noted in several other schools of this type), making what are in effect ordinary corridors. The doors leading into the quadrangle were kept locked most of the time because youths had been known to walk into, or even climb into, the quadrangle and so gain access to the classrooms. It was noted that the corridors were used for displaying some of the children's work, but the headmistress said that, since the corridors were unheated, they could not be used by groups of children except in very warm weather. (It was very warm at the time of the visit, but only one child was observed reading in one of the corridors.)

The chief complaint made by the headmistress was that infant activities were considerably curtailed because her school had to share the hall with the junior school. Although she took the whole of her school for morning assembly in the hall on two mornings a week, the

school 'seemed to have no centre'. Also, the original storage cupboards in the classrooms were not large enough – there was 'nowhere
to put anything' – and some of the smaller items of P.E. apparatus
had to be left in the corridors. The classrooms, though provided with
sinks, were without a hot-water supply, and the cloakrooms, which
were concentrated in two parts of the school, were not satisfactory
since they became too congested. Other complaints arose because of
the sloping nature of the site: there were 'stairs everywhere' and
ball games were very difficult because of the sloping playground.

It is interesting to note that this school when first built (and in
spite of the inflated numbers during its first few years) was regarded
as a 'show' school. The log book records visits from the Vice-Principal,
Method Mistress and fifty students from a nearby teacher-training
college, and other visits were made by college staff and headmistresses
from adjoining towns. The report by H.M. Inspector in 1930 stated
that the premises were 'most attractive and healthy' and added that,
in spite of the crowded conditions

> the children are carefully graded and the ample apparatus,
> allowing for individual work in all subjects, ensures satisfactory
> progress. The teachers, on the whole, work well together and
> are keen about their work, anxious to discover the best ways
> of creating happiness and brightness for the children, as well
> as ensuring a satisfactory standard of work.

A junior school of 1926

Some of the criticisms made by the infant school headmistress were
echoed by the headmaster of the adjoining junior school. In this
school, the verandas have remained unaltered, not because the headmaster is in favour of them but because he felt that enclosing them
would involve a good deal of expense in order to make unheated,
draughty corridors which would be little better than the arrangement he has now. The basic trouble, in his view, was that the original
classrooms were too small for creating activity areas, and he was
pressing the local authority to merge the veranda space with the
classrooms so that in the extra, wholly internal, space thus obtained
it would be possible to form 'activity bays' and to disperse the cloakroom accommodation (for he also disliked the centralized cloakroom
areas). He agreed that older schools were in more urgent need of
improvement than his, but thought that there was a real danger of

schools of the inter-war period also becoming slum schools if improvements were not put in hand soon.

A young woman teacher who until recently worked in this junior school made the following points about the building:

1. The classrooms opened directly on to the quadrangle so that in winter every time the doors opened the rooms became cold and papers blew about etc.

2. Moving from one room to another was a cold business as even in summer the open veranda around the quadrangle acted like a wind tunnel.

3. There was no water supply in the classrooms so that art could never be done by one group whilst the others wrote or did other academic activities. It was the same with science and maths where water was involved – all the class had to do it together because of carrying buckets of water about.

4. The walls facing into the quadrangle had a great many windows in them so that everyone could see into every other room at all times. It was rather like a peep-show. One could not be experimental and fail without every other child and member of staff knowing about it.

5. There were no extra spaces like corridors into which work could expand as it was too cold outside the classrooms for at least six months of the year.

6. The shared hall restricted the number of P.E., movement and drama lessons. Displays in the hall could, however, be seen by all the children and spark off different follow-ups.

7. The steps into the classrooms made the moving of larger equipment difficult, e.g. the T.V. trolley.

8. The garden in the quadrangle was pleasant to look at in summer, with its lawn and flowering shrubs.

9. The staffroom was near enough for all the teachers to use it at breaks, and the staff developed a unity.

A senior school of 1931

The last school to be considered in this chapter differs from those so far described in a number of respects. First, although now occupied by a junior school, it was originally designed as a new-style senior school for boys and girls over the age of eleven, as advocated in the Hadow Report of 1926. Also, this school is in a suburban area which has continued to expand since the 1930s and is therefore not in the possibly enviable position of the schools mentioned above which have been to some degree left behind by the march of events.

The original plan of the school is given in Fig. 6, which shows that it was built around an open courtyard, with classrooms (numbered 1 to 10 on the plan) on two sides, practical rooms on the third side, and the hall on the fourth. Most of the classrooms originally measured 480 square feet and were designed for forty pupils each, providing accommodation for a total of about 200 boys and 200 girls aged between eleven and fourteen (which was the official leaving age from 1921 to 1947). It will be seen that this plan differs from those for juniors and infants considered earlier in this chapter in its provision of two large practical rooms for handicraft and domestic science. It should also be noted that, although cross-ventilation was still secured by providing high-level windows on both sides of the classrooms, heated corridors and not verandas were used to provide access to the classrooms, probably because it was already being realized by the 1930s that verandas were proving unpopular with

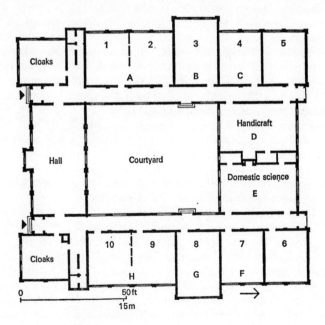

Figure 6   Senior school, built 1931, with corridors and quadrangle

teachers (or it may have been thought that open-air conditions were not so important for older children). The courtyard, instead of being made into a garden, was asphalted, which, though less agreeable to look at, gives more direct access between the two sides of the school. As with the earlier schools considered, there were internal cloak-rooms but external w.c.s.

Since the Second World War this school has been altered twice – once to make it into an infant and junior school and more recently to convert it for the use of juniors only. Of the ten original class-rooms two (numbered 5 and 6 on the plan) have been converted to inside toilets, and the classrooms numbered 1 and 2, which were originally divided by a folding partition, have become one room, as have classrooms 9 and 10 and each of the two large practical rooms. Classrooms 4 and 7 have also been enlarged by taking in part of what were originally rooms 5 and 6. In this way the building now has eight fairly large classrooms, which are shown on the plan lettered A to H. Each class now has between thirty-five and forty junior children on the roll, so that the 1931 building accommodates about 300 children compared with the 400 for which it was designed. Since, however, the school population has continued to expand in this area, four temporary classrooms have been erected in the school grounds, accommodating a further 150 children. Dining takes place in another hutted room in the grounds, which has the great advantage of freeing the hall for other activities throughout the day.

The principal difficulty mentioned by the headmaster of this school arose from the relative isolation of the temporary classrooms, which he said were 'out on a limb'. Although they were fairly near to the main building and were not occupying valuable playground space as we have noted can happen in older schools with restricted sites, they were not easy of access, especially on wet days; also, some of the temporary classrooms were without a water supply, which meant carrying water in for science, art and other subjects.

As for the main building, the headmaster thought that the en-largement of the classrooms and the provision of internal toilets had been valuable improvements, but the children were still too much confined to their own classrooms. The central courtyard could not be used much for children's activities because it was too cold during most of the year and it was also of limited use for ball-games because of the many windows facing on to it. Similarly, the corridors were rather gloomy and therefore not really suitable for displaying the children's work. The corridors were only 7 feet wide so they could not be used for group activities without impeding children passing along them in the normal way. He was, however, determined to try to 'open up' the work of the school and was discussing with his staff a new form of organization which he hoped would achieve some of the benefits obtainable in the most recent primary school buildings.

How this school is being adapted

The headmaster's plan is to divide the school into three units of 150 children, one of which will be accommodated in the temporary classrooms, and the other two in the main school (taking rooms A to D as one unit and rooms E to H as another). The three units will be for lower, middle and top juniors, with some overlapping of ages and without the use of 'streaming'. Each unit will be divided into forms who will spend three periods a day with their own teacher in one of the rooms in that unit. But for the rest of the time the children will be free to move to any of the rooms in their unit, and each room will be equipped for particular activities, e.g. mathematics, writing, quiet reading, science and 'messy' crafts. In this way the headmaster hopes that a suitable balance will be kept between class-teaching, small-group and individual work. He is well aware that his plan will only succeed with the full co-operation of the teachers and with much attention to detailed organization. For example, individual assignments will be given to the children involving the use of equipment in various rooms and proper records of work done will be kept by the staff.

The advantages which the headmaster thought would be gained by this reorganization included the following:

1. There would be more variety both for teachers and children and fuller use would be made of the specialist interests of the staff.

2. It was more economic to share equipment among 150 children than the usual class of forty, e.g. some of the children might want to use a cooker at certain times, but there was no point in having one in every room.

3. Teachers and children would be sharing the facilities provided and would be working together in an informal setting. He hoped that this would foster a co-operative spirit, so that the teachers would become a team and each unit of 150 children a community.

4. The proposed form of organization should also encourage 'active' learning. The headmaster thought that there was too much oral exposition by the teachers and copying from books by the children in

many primary schools and he preferred a system by which the teacher guided individual children, gave encouragement in the use of reference books, made suggestions if a child was not sure what to do next, and most important, did all these things *at the time* when the child really needed help on a particular point. So far as possible, the child's natural curiosity should be the pace-maker, and the teacher should use the child's questions as the starting-point for much of the work.

5. He thought that it was unreasonable to expect a child to stop being interested in one thing and change to something else at the ringing of a bell, and the proposed alteration in school organization would also allow greater flexibility in the allocation of the time available.

The proposed reorganization in this junior school has not yet been introduced, and in any case will take some time to implement. The important issues raised by the headmaster of this school will, however, be discussed later in this book, when we come to consider some of the most recent primary schools which have been designed very much with considerations of this sort in mind. Here we may note that many of the ideas put forward in the 1960s and 1970s essentially derive from those originally expressed by the progressive educationists of the 1920s and 1930s. Whether the more generous scale on which schools were designed in the inter-war period makes them easier to adapt to the more positive forms of progressive teaching now in evidence is not, however, entirely clear. On the whole it appears that the veranda and quadrangle schools were the expression of new ideas of 'open air' rather than 'open' planning, with the doctor and landscape architect, rather than the teacher and educationist, in the ascendant.

5 The corridor plan and the reaction against it

The immediate post-war situation

In the senior school of 1931 discussed in the last chapter, we noted that corridors instead of verandas were provided. It was a natural development to make corridors the standard provision in schools, especially in view of the criticisms which even before the war were being made of the verandas. In other respects, however, the schools built immediately before and after the Second World War retained the emphasis on good lighting and ventilation, with spacious sites. Detailed cost limits were not imposed on schools until 1950 and the Building Regulations of 1945 were relatively generous in laying down standards for school buildings. Many of the schools built immediately before and after the war were probably on a more lavish scale than any built from public funds before or since – lavish, that is, not necessarily in terms of the teaching facilities provided, but in terms of corridor-space, cloakrooms, playgrounds and playing fields. The corridor-plan at its most extreme point of development resulted in what is sometimes called the 'finger-plan' school, typically belonging to the late 1930s and (following the interruption of the war) the late 1940s. The plan of such a school resembled a hand with a hall and administrative rooms forming the 'palm' and the rows of classrooms the 'fingers'. Schools of this type are illustrated in a book issued in connection with an exhibition on school planning and construction held by the Royal Institute of British Architects in 1947 (*New Schools*, 1948). School plans, according to the R.I.B.A., should above all be considered 'in terms of sunlight, daylight and ventilation' and should be built 'on the principle of separation of departments [and] segregating the noisy areas from those devoted to quiet study'. It is interesting to note that these ideas for dispersing and differentiating the various parts of a school building coincided with the period when 'streaming' in the primary schools was at its height and when the pressure for places in the grammar schools was leading to further refinements in the techniques of secondary school selection.

The result of considerations of this sort was to strengthen the tendency which we noticed in the inter-war period of dispersing the classrooms and isolating one room from the next (often by building a storeroom between adjoining classrooms). The continued influence of these ideas may also be seen in the schools illustrated in Bruce Martin's *School Buildings 1945-1951*, published in 1952, and of course in a number of schools still in use today.

This type of school was not built on an extensive scale, however, because of the general shortage of materials immediately after the war. The accommodation needed for the raising of the school leaving age from fourteen to fifteen in 1947 was provided by the 'Hutted Operation for the Raising of the School-leaving Age,' which produced the numerous HORSA huts, some of which are still in use. The main drive in primary school building came a little later as a direct result of the steep increase in the birthrate immediately after the war. The peak was reached in 1947 but the birthrate had been rising since 1942 and continued at a high rate thereafter. The attention now paid to primary school building was probably unparalleled since the period following the passing of the 1870 Education Act.

The need for controls

It was clear that 'finger-plan' schools of the kind being built in some areas were far too costly both in land and materials. The 1945 Building Regulations were revised in 1951 and 1954, annual school-building programmes were introduced in 1949 and detailed cost controls a year later. The effects on school buildings may be gauged from Table V, which is based on figures given in *The Story of Post-war School Building*, 1957, p. 22. It will be seen that the minimum teaching areas laid down in 1954 were very little higher than those of 1936 and notably less, in the case of the larger schools, than those of 1945.

Table V   Teaching accommodation provided in new primary schools between 1936 and 1954

No. of form entries (F.E.) of 40 each	Minimum area of teaching accommodation in square feet provided under:		
	1936 Recommendations	1945 Regulations	1954 Regulations
Infants			
1 F.E.	2,540	2,700	2,760
2 F.E.	4,980	4,760	5,200
3 F.E.	7,020	7,256	7,080

Juniors	1936 Recommendations	1945 Regulations	1954 Regulations
1 F.E.	3,670	4,280	3,880
2 F.E.	6,230	7,125	6,260
3 F.E.	8,500	10,428	8,640

This reduction in teaching areas went hand in hand with a comparable reduction in the cost per place allowed in building new schools. The cost per place immediately after the war has been estimated at about £200 for primary school buildings. This was reduced to £170 in 1950 and to £140 in 1951, despite the continuing rise in the price of building. In 1957, when the cost per place stood at £154, the Ministry of Education was able to claim that 'the money cost of a 1956 school is about 20 per cent less than a 1949 school in spite of the rise in building costs of over 50 per cent'.

The Ministry of Education also claimed that, though the total area per child in primary and secondary schools was cut by about 40 per cent between 1949 and 1956, the amount of actual teaching space (as distinct from space taken up by administrative rooms and 'circulation') had been maintained or even increased, so that most of the saving had been on the less essential parts of the school. In *The Story of Post-war School Building*, the plans of three primary schools built in 1945-9, 1950-3 and 1954-7 were analysed (pp. 34-40) with the results shown in Table VI.

Table VI   The percentages of total floor area given over to various uses in three post-war primary schools

Date of school	Teaching accommoda- tion[a] %	Non-teaching accommodation		Area per place sq. ft.
		Circulation[b] %	Other[c] %	
1945-9	39·1	23·2	37·7	69
1950-3	46·3	20·4	33·3	54
1954-7	67·4	7·0	25·6	43

Notes   [a] Includes classrooms and assembly hall
   [b] Especially corridors
   [c] Includes dining space (where separate) and kitchen, administrative offices, cloakrooms, w.c.s etc.

As with so many official statistics of all periods, a word of caution may be needed in interpreting Table VI. We do not know, for example, how 'typical' of their respective dates these schools were, and it should also be noted that the first and second schools had separate dining rooms, which are included in the fourth column of the table, whereas in the last school the dining room and assembly hall were combined and so are included in the second column. The most significant column is probably the third, which shows a radical reduction in circulation space. How was this achieved, marking as it does a complete reversal of the earlier tendency to build schools with ever-increasing corridor-space? And how did it come about that, as so often in the past, the new stress on economy seemed to chime in perfectly with the educational and architectural ideas then current?

How economies were achieved

As to the mechanics of the operation, the reduction in cost was made not only by reducing total floor areas but also the height of rooms in new schools. Floor area was saved principally by stressing the idea of dual use. The combination of hall and dining area has already been mentioned; similarly, internal access to a classroom was often by way of another classroom, or, to put the official slant upon it, the corridor space was merged with the classroom space to provide a larger classroom which was only used for circulation on the relatively few occasions when another class was passing through it. In the main, however, it was realized that the children in most primary schools were still spending most of their time in their own classrooms, with some use of the hall for assembly, physical education and so on. Thus the chief need for circulation was between the classrooms and the hall, and the only way to make a saving in this respect was to bring the classrooms closer to the hall. The old central-hall plan represented, of course, the closest possible relationship between classrooms and hall but, as we saw earlier, it presented difficulties in lighting, ventilation and sound insulation. Broadly what happened in the 1950s and 1960s was that the classrooms were grouped around the hall, with some of them having direct access to it, but generally not so close as to be troubled by noise from the hall or to give up the advantages of good lighting and ventilation.

Architectural developments

The influence of changes in architectural styles generally also needs to be borne in mind. In the 1930s pitched roofs were tending to disappear in favour of flat roofs, parapet walls and strongly horizontal treatments. Then Gropius and Fry showed in their Cambridgeshire village colleges how a more humane environment could be obtained by the skilful grouping of the various parts of a building and by taking advantage of trees and lawns. After the war many architects reacted against what was often termed 'monumental' architecture and called for buildings which were strictly functional in design and built for the people who were actually going to use them.

An outlook of this kind is apparent in the first Building Bulletin issued by the Ministry of Education in 1949, *New Primary Schools*. This pointed out that the corridor-type of school too often resulted in 'a layout consisting of monotonous rows of parallel wings'. A school, like the human body, 'is an organism whose separate parts should be in proper relation to the whole, with all its limbs in proportion'. In the new primary schools the common centre of the building should be created with 'exciting spatial arrangements' and the class spaces should have 'an individual and domestic character'. More advantage, too, should be taken of the school site, especially if planted with trees and shrubs.

The influence of these ideas may readily be seen in the more imaginatively-designed primary schools built since 1949. The use of different colours and wall-textures, for example, can indeed make the centre of a school a visually exciting place, and the domestic character, especially of some infant school buildings, can be delightful. Whether the general run of primary schools – as distinct, that is to say, from those designed by a relatively small number of very experienced architectural teams and widely publicized in the architectural press – reach these high standards is more doubtful, but, even so, the effect of these ideas on subsequent design is clear. It has, for example, become usual to disperse the cloakroom and toilet accommodation so that it takes on a more domestic and less institutional character, and an increasing number of architects are varying the shape of the hall and classrooms in ways which the 1949 Bulletin had suggested. The reduced height of more recent primary school buildings also helps to give them a friendly and informal character.

Educational theory

Although the Ministry of Education was quick to point out that the design of the new-style primary schools took the latest developments in teaching method into account, a study of the official expositions of 'educational philosophy' in the 1950s and 1960s indicates that they were still derived essentially from the 'progressive' writers of the 1920s and 1930s. Thus the civil servants who wrote *The Story of Post-war School Building* mentioned above, after pointing out the inevitably close connection between school architecture and 'our current ideas of the aims and methods of education', went on to define these as follows (p. 2):

> We now hold that there should be different kinds of schools to
> provide for variety in the ages, aptitudes and abilities of
> children themselves and to suit local circumstances. Further,
> the post-war school should be designed to offer a wider range of
> subjects than in the past. A great emphasis is now laid on
> practical activities. Again, teachers wish to break down the class
> or form unit into several smaller working groups, each following
> a different aspect of the subject. This variety of subject and
> approach necessarily calls for new kinds of teaching materials,
> aids and equipment. Finally, we see a school no longer as a
> mere machine for giving lessons, but as a social unit concerned
> with the all-round development of boys and girls. For example,
> in practically every school there is provision for school meals
> which requires special planning by the architect.

Apart from the mention of school meals, there is very little here that could not have formed part of, say, the Hadow reports of 1931 and 1933. What was new was the more general acceptance of the ideas of the 1930s, and their actual implementation on a larger scale than before. There is no doubt, for example, that group work was much more widely practised in the primary schools of the 1950s and 1960s than before the war. Even more important, perhaps, was the interest which was taken by architects in the ideas of 'progressive' primary school teachers. That not only the syllabus but the building should be 'child-centred' was a point of view with which many architects were ready to sympathize, and one which accorded well with the new emphasis on functional building in contemporary architecture as a whole.

The role of the central government

It will be apparent from what has already been said that central control over school building has increased considerably since the Second World War. In fact, however, such control has been exercised in one form or another ever since Exchequer funds were first used to aid school buildings in 1833. This has always been through the prior approval of school plans and the fixing of certain limits to the disbursement of central funds. From 1863 there were, as we saw earlier, official Rules, which were replaced early in the present century by the Building Regulations. The Regulations of 1914 were withdrawn in 1926, reflecting no doubt the general uncertainty about school plans which prevailed following the demise of the central-hall plan and the break-up of the old system of elementary-school organization. They were replaced in 1936 not by regulations but recommendations, which were incorporated in the Board's pamphlet, *Elementary School Buildings*, to which reference has already been made. Following the passing of the 1944 Education Act, new *Standards for School Premises Regulations, 1945*, still commonly referred to as the Building Regulations, were introduced and, as we have seen, were modified in 1951 and 1954. (They were again altered in 1959 and 1969.)

The most creative post-war development in the role of the Government in school building has, however, resulted from the setting up in 1948 by the then Ministry of Education (now the Department of Education and Science) of a Development Group consisting not only of architects and quantity surveyors but also of H.M. Inspectors and administrators. This group is divided into teams which plan and carry out 'development projects' in close co-operation with selected L.E.A.s. The results of their work are published in Building Bulletins, to which some reference has already been made. Over forty of these Bulletins have been issued since 1949 and they are a very valuable source of information about new developments in school planning and design.

The administrator in charge of the Development Group at the Ministry of Education was D. H. Morrell and the organization which he established served as the model for the later Curriculum Development Group which itself developed into the Schools Council. It also provided an outstanding example of team work between architects and educationists which was taken up by several of the more progressive L.E.A.s.

Hertfordshire, Nottinghamshire and the consortia

The L.E.A. which first achieved a high reputation for its primary
school buildings was Hertfordshire County Council. This was an
area with a continuously-growing population (including four New
Towns and two L.C.C. housing estates) and one where the shortage
of traditional building materials and craftsmen was particularly acute
because of the competing demands of housing and light industry.
Yet one hundred new schools were completed by 1954 and the
second hundred by 1961. The basis of this success lay in the use of
standardized components which were mass produced in factories and
then assembled speedily on the site (so avoiding many of the usual
delays owing to bad weather which occur with traditional methods
of construction).

The new Hertfordshire schools were planned on a grid system,
that is, in units of a standard size so that doors, windows, wall-panels
etc. could also be standardized. The grid square used at first was
8 feet 3 inches, later reduced to 3 feet 4 inches and then to 2 feet 8
inches. The smaller grid permitted greater flexibility in arranging
the components, e.g. the width of a window could be 2 feet 8 inches,
5 feet 4 inches, 8 feet, and so on. These components were fitted into
a light steel framework, so that the final result was a building with
high standards of lighting and ventilation and of a domestic, informal
character, which many educationists as well as architects considered
was particularly suitable for primary schools. That it was also possible to achieve aesthetic merit was demonstrated in 1951 when a
Hertfordshire primary school was awarded an R.I.B.A. medal, the
first time such an award had been made to a building constructed
mainly of standardized factory-made components. It was in large
measure because of the financial economies achieved in buildings of
this kind that the Ministry of Education was, as we saw earlier, able
to reduce the cost limits for schools at a time when building costs
generally were rising. (For further details see *Building for Education,
1948-1961*, County Hall, Hertford, 1962.)

Many of the lessons learnt in Hertfordshire were applied in Nottinghamshire and other areas. Here the need for a light and flexible
type of building was accentuated by the problems presented by
mining subsidence. The traditional solution of inserting heavy concrete foundations was expensive and not always effective, but it was
found that a spring-loaded light steel framework could adapt to sur-
face movement caused by underground mining, and extensive use
was also made of tile cladding which could move like the scales of a

fish when the building itself moved. Other authorities with mining-subsidence problems joined with Nottinghamshire in 1957 to form a Consortium of Local Authorities Special Programme (CLASP), which developed new methods of standardization, bulk-buying and 'serial tendering' (by which particular components were mass-produced by selected firms over a longer period and for a larger market than was possible with the old practice of inviting tenders for each school individually). This system, too, involved planning schools on a grid pattern, but again it proved capable of producing buildings of architectural merit, as was shown when a CLASP primary school was awarded the *gran premio con menzione speciale* at the twelfth Milan Triennale in 1960. (For further details see Building Bulletin No. 19, *The Story of CLASP*, 1961.)

The advantages of co-operation between L.E.A.s in the design of schools led to the setting up of several more consortia in the 1960s. The initial association with problems of mining subsidence which led to the formation of CLASP has disappeared but the benefits derived from joint planning and purchasing have been widely recognized. Details of the work of the various consortia, which have also adopted somewhat cryptic abbreviated titles, may be studied in an interesting series of articles which appeared in the journal *Education*, as detailed below.

Date of article	Name of consortium	Full title and date of foundation
28.3.69	ONWARD	Organization of North West Authorities for Rationalized Design (1966)
25.4.69	CLASP	Consortium of Local Authorities Special Programme (1957)
27.6.69	EASC	East Anglian Standing Conference (1964)
25.7.69	SEAC	South Eastern Architects' Collaboration (1963)
29.8.69	MACE	Metropolitan Architectural Consortium for Education (1966)
28.11.69	CLAW	Consortium of Local Authorities in Wales (1962)
30.1.70	CMB	Consortium for Method Building (1963)
27.2.70	SCOLA	Second Consortium of Local Authorities (1961)

Two case-studies of the 1950s

Before we go on to deal with the most recent developments in primary school design, it is worth pausing briefly to consider two schools which, from the architectural point of view, are less enterprising than those considered above, but which are more typical of the large number of primary schools actually built in the 1950s to cope with the first wave of expansion made necessary by the rising birth-rate. These two schools were for infant and junior children respectively and were built between 1955 and 1957 on the same site on a new housing estate in a large industrialized town. Use was made of an earlier type of standardized steel frame, but with a good deal of brickwork and other traditional materials. The plan of the infant school is shown in Fig. 7 and from the design point of view we may say that this represents, like many other schools of the 1950s, an intermediate style, midway between the earlier finger-type plans and the more compact designs of the kind advocated in Building Bulletin No. 1 and actually being built in Hertfordshire.

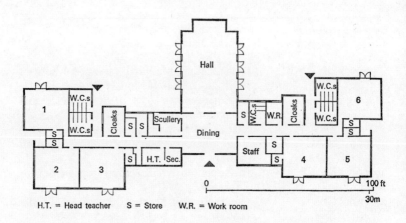

Figure 7 Infant school, built 1955. The classrooms are numbered 1 to 6 and each has a store adjoining it. The entrance hall is also used for dining, and the corridors are lit by windows in the roof.

The school shown in Fig. 7 was planned before the impact of the new policy of cutting down on circulation space had been fully felt, but the long corridors usual in the immediate post-war schools have been replaced by two shorter lengths of corridor which serve three classrooms on each side of the hall. There is access to the w.c.s from inside the building (unlike most pre-war schools) and the sanitary accommodation, like that for coats, has been split into two. Each classroom has an area of 600 square feet and a small store room and was designed for forty pupils (making a total of 240). A dining room separate from the hall has been provided, though it also serves as a 'crush hall', i.e. as part of the main entrance to the school. There is a pleasant staffroom, a small workroom and a scullery, in addition to rooms for the head teacher and secretary. Since this building is of single-storey construction, it has been possible to light the corridors by means of windows in the roof. All the classrooms face south and all but one of them can be cross-ventilated.

A constant difficulty in planning new primary schools is to take proper account of the long-term population trends in the area. Thus, when this school was first opened, it was severely overcrowded and use had also to be made of hutted classrooms in the playground. In 1970, however, the number of children on the roll had declined to 152, arranged in four classes of thirty-eight. One of the original classrooms is now used as a library and another as a room into which children from any class can go for making large models etc. The school works an 'integrated day' and the headmistress has adopted a modified form of 'vertical grouping': i.e., there are two classes with both five and six-year-old children in them and two with six and seven-year-old children. She did not think that it was desirable to mix five and seven-year-old children, since the teacher of such a class would have to give too much time to the youngest children and the seven-year-olds would not be sufficiently 'stretched'.

This headmistress had clearly established very good relationships with the parents and staff. She did not think that team-teaching was necessary since her relatively small staff freely exchanged ideas in the staffroom and were always ready to help each other. Her only real criticisms of the building were that the flat roofs still let in water (a very common complaint), that the hall was inadequately heated and that the corridors were gloomy. Although the children could go to either of the 'spare' classrooms when necessary, they generally needed to be nearer to their own teachers and so painting etc, was often done in the corridors (where painting-easels, various displays and several pets in boxes had led to a certain amount of congestion).

At this school there seemed to be ample space, though it is interesting to note that even with classrooms of 600 square feet the children's work had overflowed into the corridors. The still somewhat institutional character of the building had been alleviated by colourful displays, not only in the classrooms and corridors but in the crush hall and main hall. In the adjoining junior school, where the design of the building was similar but where the numbers were larger (because children from some of the crowded central schools were being transported to it every day), the institutional character of the building was much more marked and the impression of so many standardized classroom-boxes remained dominant.

Further comments about a school of the 1950s

Some comments from the headmistress of a six-class infant and junior school built in another town in 1956 are also worth quoting. Her school is of very similar plan to that just described but it accommodates 251 children instead of the 240 for which it was designed. Her first point is one which would be echoed by many teachers in this type of school:

> The whole of one side facing the road is glazed from a
> level of 2 feet 6 inches above the floor. The natural lighting
> afforded by this extensive use of glass gives the classrooms
> a light, airy appearance but, since all these windows face
> south-east, the amount of full sunshine during the summer is
> overpowering and the venetian blinds effectively prevent cross-
> ventilation as many of the windows are difficult to open
> when the blinds are in use.

This headmistress also remarks that the classrooms are 'completely self-contained units' so that 'when the classroom doors are closed each room is effectively sealed off'. Some use is made of the corridors and the hall for group activities and the head's room is also used by groups making music, listening to tape-recordings or quietly reading. But the problem of the classrooms remains:

> The classes are very easily shut off from seeing what others
> are doing by virtue of the windowless walls and doors to the
> corridors. This tends to reinforce the old ideas of formalism
> and to inhibit a more flexible approach. The design of

the building insists that all the teaching areas are large, exposed and bounded by straight lines. The difficulty lies in finding enough intimate group-working places that do not spell out uniformity and that give a child the chance to be seen as an individual.

6 Compact and open plans

A question of terminology

The title of this chapter may well appear to contain an internal contradiction. The contradiction is, however, more apparent than real. From the architectural point of view, the move to reduce circulation space which began in the 1950s continued strongly into the 1960s, and in most recent primary schools the classrooms have entered into very close relationship with each other and with the hall, with the result that very compact plans have been produced. From the educational point of view, there has been a marked tendency to break out of the traditional classroom areas and to create other teaching spaces, which has had the effect of 'opening up' the building. The merging of these architectural and educational aspects of design has meant that in many of the most recent primary schools it would be more accurate to describe the entire school (except for the kitchen, head's room and staffroom – and sometimes not even these) as one large teaching area.

In many places these changes in school design have been accompanied by more flexible methods of internal organization, including the abandonment of the old type of timetable in favour of an 'integrated day', the introduction of 'vertical grouping' across the age-ranges and 'non-streaming' across the ability-ranges. The children work in groups of varying size and the teachers work together as a team. Often the groups belonging to one class of forty children work at entirely different activities, and not simply at different aspects of the same subject, which was what had earlier been meant by 'group work'. Groups from different classes also intermingle for various activities.

Although primary schools built on the new pattern form a marked contrast to those built before the Second World War, the essential rationale which underlies them may nevertheless again be traced back to an earlier period. The nursery schools pioneered by Margaret Mc-Millan anticipated many of the developments of the 1960s, and the germ of what has come to be known as 'open planning' may be detected, for example, in the views of one witness quoted in the 1933 report, *Infant and Nursery Schools* (p. 161):

> The ideal Infant School is not a classroom but a playground,
> that is to say, not a limited space enclosed by four walls and
> a ceiling, but an open area ... where the interests natural
> to this biological stage of growth can be stimulated
> and pursued.

This opinion, which may in turn be traced to the nineteenth-century pioneers of infant education, is, indeed, an even more extreme expression of 'open planning' than many teachers, especially of children above the infant age, were prepared to accept in the 1960s. We will find that the majority of primary schools built in the 1960s were designed on what might better be called the 'semi-open' principle, that is, with a good deal of shared teaching space, but with the classroom-areas still well defined. We will also find that some teachers working in semi-open and open-plan schools are not entirely happy with the new arrangements.

The school at Amersham

A prototype of what we have called the semi-open primary school was fully publicized in the Ministry of Education's Building Bulletin No. 16 (*Development Projects: Junior School, Amersham*, 1958). This was an eight-class junior school with the classrooms arranged in two groups of four. The individual classrooms were quite distinct but each group of four was arranged in such a way as to allow easy access from one room to another. Two of the classrooms shared a practical space and two others were built with large bays for practical work. The dining area was also used for music and had direct access to the hall, which was square (instead of oblong) in shape and provided the internal link between the two main groups of classrooms. The ground plan reproduced in the Bulletin also shows how the small courtyards created by the arrangement of the rooms were set out with trees and a pond so that in fine weather much of the outside area could be used for teaching purposes.

This Bulletin also has an interesting discussion of the relative advantages of prefabricated and brick structures, pointing out that the former were unlikely to account for more than a quarter of any national school-building programme, for which reason the school at Amersham was designed to demonstrate that brick-built schools could be as financially competitive as prefabricated schools. (Since this date, the proportion of 'system-built' schools in the annual building programmes has risen to about 40 per cent, though discussion about the pros and cons of 'system building', including the aesthetic as well as the financial aspect, has continued in the architectural press.) Another notable feature of this project was the importance attached to furniture design, since it was realized that the shape and size of a room ought to be determined not only by the activities taking place

in it but also by reference to the actual pieces of furniture and equipment which it will have to accommodate. Illustrated in the Bulletin,
for example, are new designs for stackable chairs and movable locker
units, all intended to increase the flexibility possible in using the
building.

A *junior school of 1963*

One of the many schools built during the 1960s with similar considerations in mind may now be described in the light of the comments made by the staff at present using it. (Further plans of this
type may be studied in Building Bulletin No. 23, *Primary School
Plans*, 1964.) The school selected for discussion is, like Amersham, an
eight-class junior school, and the plan of it is given in Fig. 8. It will
be seen that the classrooms are arranged in pairs and that each classroom is provided with separate coat-hanging and toilet facilities. Each
pair of classrooms has a 'shared space' for practical activities; two of

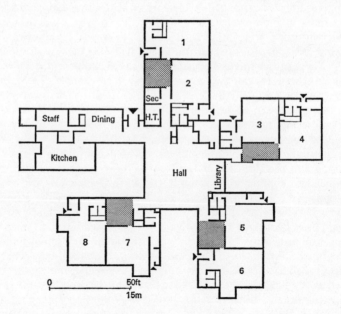

Figure 8   Junior school, built 1963. Practical areas stippled.

these spaces are also used for dining, for which reason the adjoining classrooms have been provided with additional bays for practical work. There is a recess for the library on one side of the hall, and it will be noted that there are no corridors in this school, access to the classrooms being by way of the shared spaces.

The headmaster of this school declared himself to be completely opposed to 'progressive methods' in primary education and he was also very critical of his new school building. One of his main complaints was that the splitting up of the cloakrooms and dining areas made supervision unnecessarily difficult. Since there were no outside toilets, children had to come into the school during breaks and at lunch-time, and in fact he kept several of the toilet areas locked at these times. (One of the class-teachers also said that it was hard to supervise the toilet areas, in which children tended to 'mess about'.) The headmaster considered that the ventilation was 'poor throughout', a point also mentioned by one of the class-teachers who said that his room 'got like an oven' when there was no breeze outside. (It is certainly true that the principles of cross-ventilation usual in the inter-war schools have been modified in this school because of the grouping of the classrooms.) The headmaster also criticized the proximity of the library to the hall (he had in fact had it closed in) and added that the noise problem was much greater than in the old central-hall-type school from which he had moved.

It was clear from talking to the class-teachers that much of the work at this school was of a formal character and was almost entirely based on the full class unit. The teacher in one of the classrooms with a bay remarked that it was useful 'for sending nuisances into' and another said that he could think of no use for the shared space outside his room. One of these areas was being used for remedial teaching and another for needlework: in only one was an unsupervised group at work. At the time of the visit – towards the end of a summer term – the dual desks were mainly arranged in groups, but several of the teachers said that they were not always arranged like this. One teacher of a fourth-year class said that it was essential to have the desks in rows at certain times so that 'everyone can see the board when new work is being explained', i.e. he regarded his class as a homogeneous group. Another teacher of a fourth-year class said that, because of the eleven-plus examination, it was necessary for the children to 'get into the way of not speaking' when they worked, or they might be disqualified during the examination. She added that it was easier for the children to 'do what they liked' if they were arranged in groups and that 'B children' in particular found it hard to organize their time and tended to 'wander about not doing anything'. The teacher of a first-year class said that she usually arranged the children in rows at the beginning of the school year so that she could get to know their names and 'sort out their abilities', after which they were arranged in what she called 'ability groups' in the morning (for work in the basic subjects) and 'activity groups' in the afternoon for art, craft etc. The same distinction between formal work in the morning and informal work in the afternoon was made by the teacher of a second-year class.

This school has a high reputation for its 'eleven-plus results', as well as being known locally for its marked interest in rural science. One could hardly find, however, a clearer example of the ideas of the staff running counter to those which inspired the design of the building.

The move towards open planning

The Development Group of the Department of Education and Science, in collaboration with a number of L.E.A.s, designed new primary schools at Finmere in Oxfordshire and Great Ponton in Lincolnshire (described in the revised edition of Building Bulletin No. 3, *Village Schools*, 1961) and in South-east London (see Building Bulletin No. 36, *Eveline Lowe Primary School, London*, 1967). The design of all these schools was based on careful observation of the work going on in a number of existing primary schools where (as in some of the examples quoted earlier in this book) the teachers were trying to adapt their buildings to new methods of teaching. The designers of the Eveline Lowe School, for example, were impressed by the variety of activities which went on in some primary schools and, it may be noted, by no means only in those of the most recent construction. They concluded that teachers in such schools were expanding their activities in ways that were causing the distinction between teaching and non-teaching areas to disappear. In addition, in the village schools especially, they noted that rigid divisions by age or ability were rarely imposed, because of the smaller numbers and the family atmosphere of the kind described in chapter 2 of this book.

In other schools, however, formal classroom teaching was continuing in traditional fashion. The Development Group felt that the large square or oblong classrooms characteristic of most post-war primary schools did little to encourage teachers to use the space available for the full range of group activities. The provision of practical

areas, whether as a bay in each classroom or as a shared space between classrooms (as was usual in the new schools of the early 1960s)
did not seem to go far enough. In schools where group activities were
being practised the distinction between practical and non-practical
activities seemed to have little meaning and every available space,
whatever its original purpose, had often been pressed into service.
What gave these spaces character was the nature of the particular
activities going on in them and the kind of equipment kept in them.

The basic idea therefore adopted in the Eveline Lowe School as
actually built was to create different spaces for different activities and
to give them architectural expression either by providing movable
furniture or by forming bays and other spaces of varying size, shape
and floor-finish. There were still rooms where groups of forty children could, for example, listen to one of the teachers read a story, but
a number of other spaces were provided and inter-connected in such
a way that smaller groups of children could use a much more extensive and interesting area than would have been possible under the old
arrangement of separate classrooms.

Many of the ideas which lay behind the design of the Eveline Lowe
School also found expression in the Plowden Report of 1967. The
Eveline Lowe School had been designed for 320 children with an age-
range of three and a half to nine years, i.e. spanning the usual ages of
transfer from nursery to infant and from infant to junior school,
and the building was also designed to encourage parents and other
adults to use it. This accorded well with the Plowden Report's stress
on the role of parents and ancillary staff and with its treatment of the
differential rate of children's physical and emotional development
which suggested that greater flexibility is needed in arranging the
various stages of a child's education. The Eveline Lowe School is in
fact discussed in the Plowden Report (ch. 28) and other plans are given
there of the radically new kind of primary school building which is
being evolved.

Let us therefore now consider two such schools and the reactions of
the staff to the new patterns of organization which are inevitably
implied.

An open-plan infant school of 1968

This school, the plan of which is given in Fig. 9, was built in 1968
as an infant school with six classes arranged in two groups of three
on each side of the hall. The basic layout may therefore be said to

resemble the plan of the infant school of 1955, shown in Fig. 7. The differences between the two plans are, however, more notable than the similarities. Thus the hall in the 1968 school is fully integrated into the design and what in earlier designs would have been called the 'classrooms' have been divided up into smaller areas and arranged to form an open courtyard of irregular shape and easy of access from the covered teaching areas. Open verandas (but of shorter lengths and in more sheltered positions than in most inter-war schools) act as intermediate teaching spaces between the covered and uncovered areas of the school. The verandas can be used for such 'messy' activities as sand- and water-play, while the courtyard is an open play area for climbing and for particularly noisy activities such as hammering wood. In short, the whole of the veranda and courtyard area has been designed as an extension of the interior teaching activities.

Inside the school, the contrast with earlier plans is even more marked. The class bases consist of small rooms (numbered one to six on the plan), which though much smaller than conventional classrooms are each large enough for forty children to sit on the carpeted

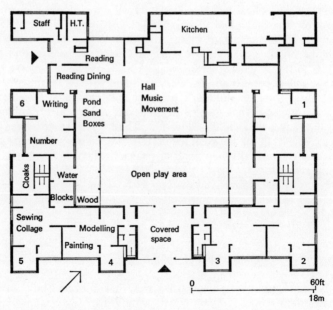

Figure 9　Open-plan infant school, built 1968

floor and listen to a story, as well as giving every child and teacher a clear sense of identity (since all have their 'home bases'). This arrangement makes it possible for each group of three classes, or 120 children, in each wing of the building to use the whole of the space in their wing for most of the day. The hall is shared for P.E. and music by the children in both wings, as is the open courtyard in the centre of the school. The children in both wings of the school also mix for morning assembly and dining, and, of course, at other times in the school grounds. All the teachers at this school were enthusiastic about the building, which seemed to be providing them with everything they wanted. As the headmistress remarked, 'we think that the building is only being properly used when it is fully used', and she added that the great advantage of the building was that it provided opportunities for the children and teachers to express their interests and abilities to the full.

The detailed organization of the school is best understood by considering the activities which take place in one wing of the building accommodating 120 children. Certain parts of each wing are equipped for particular activities, as shown on the left-hand side of Fig. 9. It will be seen that there are distinct but closely interconnected areas for quiet reading, for writing and number work, for 'dry' crafts (sewing, collage, model-making etc.) and 'wet' crafts (painting, modelling with clay etc.). The tables in the reading area are also suitable for dining, which is unobtrusively organized on a group or 'family' basis. Apart from the occasions, usually at the beginning and end of the morning and afternoon sessions, when the children are in their home bases, they are free to work at any of these activities and the three teachers also move freely throughout the whole of their wing of the building. The hall is available for P.E. activities in the morning and music in the afternoon and the children are given considerable freedom to decide for themselves when they want to go to the hall.

A common criticism of open-plan schools is that the children too easily become 'lost'. This did not seem to be the case in this school because, as explained above, each child had his own base and his own teacher to give him a feeling of security. A check was also kept on the work done by the children through the regular discussions which they were able to have with their teachers in their base rooms and through a system of work-books which the teachers marked. It also seemed that the children were perfectly well able to establish friendly contact with the other teachers in their wing, and indeed with the whole staff, both teaching and non-teaching. (There were also a number of infant helpers and students in this school at the time of the visit and the distinction just made between 'teaching' and 'non-teaching' appeared in fact to be quite inappropriate in this context.)

As may be said to follow inevitably from the details already given, the organization of this school was entirely innocent of any notion of arranging the children by year-group or by ability, however defined. Some visitors to schools of this type, however, allege that conditions become chaotic and the children's work too disconnected, with the result that grounding in the 'basic subjects' (usually defined very narrowly) is neglected. And where – as in the case of the school just described – the children appear to be working happily and purposefully, it is often said that the better schools of this kind attract particularly talented staff and that the average teacher could not do it. Nobody who has seen a well-designed and properly-organized school of this type in operation can doubt that considerable teaching skills are required. But what seem to be needed are not so much those indefinable qualities associated with brilliant individual performances as a grasp of essential principles and a capacity to play one's part in a complex teaching situation, for which specific training can be given. Ancillary staff can also make a real contribution and may be regarded in the same light as the para-medical staff who support the work of the modern doctor.

An open-plan junior school of 1969

It will be recalled that the headmistress in the infant school of 1955 described in our last chapter did not believe in teaching five and seven-year-old children together because the seven-year-olds would not be sufficiently 'stretched'. In the infant school of 1968 mentioned above, it was also noted that at the time of the visit (towards the end of the school year) some of the seven-year-old children due to be transferred to the junior school had been taken out of their groups in order to 'get them ready for the juniors'. There has been sufficient criticism from junior schools of the alleged lack of grounding (and especially lack of reading ability) in infant schools to make infant teachers sensitive on the point. How far this criticism, as applied to open-plan as distinct from other kinds of infant schools, is valid remains to be proved, but it certainly seems to be the case that many of the ideas which have successfully entered the infant schools have been received with less enthusiasm when applied to schools for older children.

Some L.E.A.s, in an attempt to 'open up' the junior school in ways comparable with what has already been achieved in the infant school, have built junior schools of more open design, though generally still retaining the separate and relatively large classroom-spaces which have been a regular feature of new primary schools since about 1890. The plan of one such school is given in Fig. 10, which shows an eight-class junior school with a large, shared practical space and a library/resource area adjoining it. This 'additional' provision has been achieved, at any rate in part, by a slight reduction in classroom areas (the majority of which are under 600 square feet, compared, for example, with 600 square feet or over provided in the schools shown in Figs 7 and 8). Another point of interest is that the practical space, because of its central position, is mainly lit by windows in the roof which are provided in large numbers and are only possible in a single-storey building (though the modification of the minimum daylight factor which the 1969 amendment to the Building Regulations permits will no doubt lead to greater use in future of what is termed 'permanent supplementary artificial lighting of interiors', P.S.A.L.I.).

The generous provision of practical space and its concentration in one central area (unlike the dispersed arrangement shown in Fig. 8)

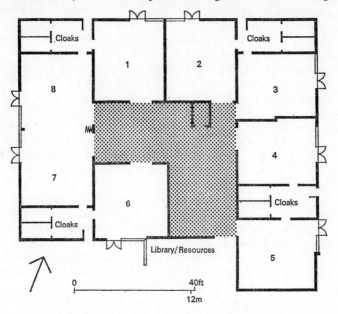

Figure 10 Open-plan junior school, built 1969. Practical area stippled.

produces a plan more like the old central-hall layout than any so far considered, but it should be noted that a separate hall (not shown on the plan and also used for dining) has been provided and that the practical area is not one barren open space but has been interestingly designed to house the equipment needed for music, science, the keeping of pets and plants and so on, i.e. it is an extension of the 'activity areas' which many primary school teachers have been creating in spare corners of their schools in the ways described in earlier chapters of this book. The large openings instead of doors between the classrooms and the practical space are meant to improve the flow of activities, and classrooms seven and eight have a movable partition between them, designed to be easily opened in order to extend the practical activities into that entire area.

This school has only recently started work and it would therefore be unreasonable to make any dogmatic statements about the way that the plan is working out in practice. Certain difficulties have, however, already been encountered. The headmaster and his staff, although keen to share the excellent equipment provided and sympathetic to the 'progressive' approach, have made modifications in the organization of the school and the use to which the building is being put which were not envisaged by its designers. Thus the movable partition has remained closed and the library area is considered to be too far away from the class bases to use for its intended purpose, books being kept in part of the practical area. The main difficulty mentioned by the headmaster, however, was that it was unrealistic to expect eight teachers to co-operate in using the practical area – not because they were by nature unco-operative (quite the reverse) – but because the side-effects of even one practical activity were often enough to 'freeze' the whole area. For example, when it was decided to hold a mock election, a voting booth had to be erected immediately in front of the science bench, so preventing its use for science; when musical instruments were being played, it was not possible to read quietly in the adjoining area, so that music had in fact been transferred to the hall; similarly, woodwork was too noisy and was carried on in what was (temporarily) a spare classroom. He therefore thought that it would have been better to have separated the noisy and quiet areas and to have divided up the practical space in such a way that only two or three teachers need share each 'parcel' of it at any given time.

In spite of the limitations which this building already seems to be imposing on the school, the staff's enthusiasm for group work and for a variety of activities remained unabated. The headmaster pointed out that with formal class-teaching a child can easily 'switch off' and, if he finishes a piece of work before the others, the usual practice is either to give him more of the work which he has already mastered, or to tell him to wait until the others catch up. With group work, however, the child can give more of himself to the task. There was also no reason why every child in a class should be doing the same kind of activity at the same time: division into groups made for a more varied syllabus and enabled the teacher to share both his time and the school's equipment more sensibly (e.g., it would be very inefficient to ask a class of forty children to carry out a local historical study all at the same time – the teacher would need to brief a small group to investigate one aspect of it, perhaps including a visit to the local church, and other groups at other times could study different aspects of the subject). On the architectural arrangements provided, the headmaster remarked that there was no reason *per se* to teach outside the classrooms: a teacher would only be justified in moving groups outside if additional resources had been made available elsewhere. The headmaster was, however, far from being opposed to the provision of practical and other spaces outside the classrooms, and though in the present instance they seem to have been badly arranged, the great potential advantage of a plan of this kind is that it provides covered teaching space additional to the classrooms and hall, which is in marked contrast to virtually all earlier types of primary school.

Some conclusions

We noted at the beginning of this chapter that the considerably reduced circulation space now provided in schools seemed to accord well with the idea of using every part of the building as teaching space. It would be a mistake, however, to minimize the problems involved in this. Many of the new developments in primary education need additional space, and the cost limits imposed by the Government often make it very difficult to provide what is required. It is significant that the area per place of the Eveline Lowe School was over 45 square feet at a time when the national average for primary schools was 41 square feet, and, even then, several of the projected rooms had to be omitted. The net cost per place for primary schools in 1970 was £227, little more than it was twenty years ago before the cost-place system was introduced.

This financial pressure appears to operate particularly unfavourably for junior schools, where not only are the children physically larger but their activities require increasingly complicated equipment. 'Home bases' of the kind provided in the infant school of 1968, described above, are also needed for juniors, but it is generally assumed that these bases have to be very much larger in junior schools than infant schools. With present cost controls, this means that the other teaching spaces which can be allowed are strictly limited. Greater flexibility seems to be possible in 'middle schools' but these are still mainly at the design stage. Meanwhile, further analysis seems to be called for of the kind of activities which are best done in groups of thirty to forty children and those which would be more efficiently catered for by the provision of smaller, more specialized areas, bearing in mind the amount of supervision required, the current teacher/pupil ratios and the possibility of ancillary help.

More work is also clearly needed on the best ways of interrelating the 'base' and other areas, particularly in schools for older children. In this connection, more account might be taken of the historical antecedents of activity methods, which seem often to have worked best in village schools with small classes, and in buildings with plenty of odd corners where mess and noise do not interfere with the quieter activities of the school. One also has the impression (which would need to be checked) that these methods work better with infants and juniors in the same building than with juniors alone. On the technical side, the problems of lighting, heating, ventilation and sound-insulation will continue to need much attention, as is indicated in Professor Hopkinson's environmental appraisal of the Eveline Lowe School given at the end of Building Bulletin No. 36. (See also the article by David Medd in *Trends in Education*, No. 15, July 1969.)

Since it seems likely that many more schools of this kind are going to be built, there is an urgent need for detailed studies of the internal organization of open-plan schools, and impartial assessments should also be made of the advantages and disadvantages for children and teachers of working in what for this country are relatively new conditions, at any rate above the infant level. It would probably be especially helpful if such studies concerned themselves not only with the method but the content of the learning which takes place. In more general terms, it is to be hoped that school architecture and organization – which, as we have seen, are inextricably interwoven with each other and with the curriculum – will increasingly receive the attention due to them from teachers as well as architects, and that more time will be given to the many aspects of this subject in students' courses.

One other general feature which has emerged from this study is the time-lag apparent in the introduction of new designs. In part this has been the result of the diversity of educational provision which, particularly in the earlier period, has led to certain local authorities taking the lead and others lagging behind. Even for the post-war period, as some of the data given by Peter Manning seem to suggest (*The Primary School*, 1967), one can argue that a comparatively few 'show' schools have had all the publicity and that the general standard of primary school building has not been good. In any case, we have noted that the 'show' school of one generation can become the 'slum' school of the next.

Another major problem is the educational back-log – not only the many old primary schools which are still in use but the apparently even more permanent traditional attitudes which some teachers display. Old buildings are not always as bad inside as one expects, nor are 'traditional' teachers without their sterling qualities. There is, however, a real problem which will have to be faced as we move into the 1970s from building primary schools for new pupils (and therefore new staff) to replacing old buildings to rehouse existing children and staff. How will teachers react to open-plan principles when they come right into the school? Are the current examples of open-planning the best which can be devised to express the opinions which we hold about the way children learn? And are those opinions sufficiently articulated to withstand the criticisms which people both outside and inside the schools will be only too ready to make?

Note

In March 1971 the net cost place limit for primary schools was increased to £257. Although this took account of the inflation in building costs over the previous twelve months, it allowed no extra margin. At the same time, the cost place limit for middle schools was increased to £342 and that for secondary schools to £457. (Details in *Administrative Memorandum* No. 3/71, issued by the Department of Education and Science, 22 March 1971.)

Suggestions for further reading

The chief sources of detailed information about school buildings are the architectural and technical journals (and the journal *Education*, which has monthly sections on educational building). A number of books have also been written on the subject, though again mainly from the technical angle. In the list below only the major pre-war publications are given, with a selection of current literature, confined to books with at least one section on elementary or primary school buildings in Britain. Since changes in this field are rapid, the books below are listed in order of publication. The place of publication is London unless otherwise stated. B.B. stands for Building Bulletin.

ROBSON, E. R., *School Architecture*, Murray, 1874.
(Robson was Architect to the London School Board.)
CLAY, F., *Modern School Buildings*, Batsford, 1902 (2nd ed., 1906).
(Clay was Architect to the Board of Education.)
ROBSON, P. A., *School-planning*, Nicholson-Smith, 1911.
CLAY, F., *Modern School Buildings*, Batsford, 1929.
(The 3rd ed. of the 1902 book, completely rewritten.)
BOARD OF EDUCATION, Report of the Consultative Committee, *The Primary School*, H.M.S.O., 1931, ch.9.
   Report of the Consultative Committee, *Infant and Nursery Schools*, H.M.S.O., 1933, ch. 8.
   Educational Pamphlet No. 107, *Elementary School Buildings*, H.M.S.O., 1936.
WRIGHT, H. M. & GARDNER-MEDWIN, R., *The Design of Nursery and Elementary Schools*, Architectural Press, 1938.
(Includes examples of schools abroad.)
ROYAL INSTITUTE OF BRITISH ARCHITECTS, *New Schools*, R.I.B.A., 1948.
MINISTRY OF EDUCATION, B.B.1, *New Primary Schools*, H.M.S.O., 1949.
STILLMAN, C. G. & CLEARY, R. C., *The Modern School*, Architectural Press, 1949. (Includes examples of schools abroad.)
MINISTRY OF EDUCATION, B.B. 6, *Primary School Plans*, H.M.S.O., 1951.
MARTIN, B., *School Buildings 1945-1951*, Lockwood, 1952.
(Includes examples of schools abroad.)
GODFREY, J. A. & CLEARY, R. C., *School Design and Construction*, Architectural Press, 1953.
WEST RIDING EDUCATION COMMITTEE, *Ten Years of Change*, Wakefield: The Committee, 1953, ch. 7.

MINISTRY OF EDUCATION, *The Story of Post-war School Building*,
H.M.S.O., 1957.
  B.B. 16, *Development Projects: Junior School, Amersham*,
  H.M.S.O., 1958.
MORRELL, D. H. & POTT, A., *Britain's New Schools*, Longmans for
the British Council, 1960.
(Morrell was in charge of the Development Group at the Ministry
of Education.)
MINISTRY OF EDUCATION, B.B. 19, *The Story of CLASP*, H.M.S.O.,
1961.
  B.B. 3 (rev. ed.), *Village Schools*, H.M.S.O., 1961.
PARLIAMENT, Select Committee on Estimates, *School Building*,
8th report ... session 1960-61, H.M.S.O., 1961.
(A mine of information about school building at this period.)
ROTH, A., *The New School*, 3rd ed., Zurich : Girsberger, 1961.
(Includes some British examples.)
HERTFORDSHIRE EDUCATION COMMITTEE, *Building for Education
1948-61*, Hertford : The Committee, 1962.
NURSERY SCHOOL ASSOCIATION, *The New Nursery School: An
Appraisal of Current Design*, N.S.A., 1962.
THE 1963 CAMPAIGN FOR EDUCATION, *School Building. A Survey of
the Present Programme and its Limitations*, 1963.
HARRIS, A. N., *The Daventry Live Project*, Northampton : The
County Council, 1963.
(The building of a new primary school at Daventry, Northants.)
MINISTRY OF EDUCATION, B.B. 21, *Remodelling Old Schools*,
H.M.S.O., 1963.
NATIONAL UNION OF TEACHERS. *The State of our Schools*, N.U.T.,
1963.
MINISTRY OF EDUCATION, B.B. 23, *Primary School Plans. A Second
Selection*, H.M.S.O., 1964.
DEPARTMENT OF EDUCATION & SCIENCE, *The School Building Survey
1962*, H.M.S.O., 1965.
  B.B. 35, *New Problems in School Design. Middle Schools*,
  H.M.S.O., 1966.
NATIONAL UNION OF TEACHERS, *School of the Future*, N.U.T., 1966.
OTTO, K., *School Buildings*, Iliffe, 1966, vol. I.
(Includes some British examples.)
DEPARTMENT OF EDUCATION & SCIENCE, Report of the Central
Advisory Council for Education (England), *Children and their
Primary Schools*, H.M.S.O., 1967, vol. I, ch. 28.
  Report of the Central Advisory Council for Education (Wales),

Primary Education in Wales, H.M.S.O., 1967, ch. 26.

B.B. 36, *Eveline Lowe Primary School, London*, H.M.S.O., 1967.

EAST RIDING EDUCATION COMMITTEE, *The Condition of the Primary Schools in the East Riding of Yorkshire*, Beverley : The Committee, 1967.

MANNING, P., (ed.) *The Primary School: An Environment for Education*, Pilkington Research Unit, Department of Building Science, Liverpool University, 1967.
(One of the few evaluations of recent primary school building.)

DEPARTMENT OF EDUCATION & SCIENCE, Design Note 1, *Building for Nursery Education*, Architects & Buildings Branch, 1968.

LEVIN, P. H. & BRUCE, A. J., *The Location of Primary Schools*, Watford : Building Research Station, 1968 (Current Papers, 39/68).

BLISHEN, E. (ed), *The School that I'd Like*, Penguin, 1969.
(One of the few attempts to discover children's reactions, though mainly in secondary schools.)

MASON, S. C. (ed.), *In our Experience*, Longman, 1970, ch. 1.

TAYLOR, G. (ed.), *The Teacher as Manager*, National Council for Educational Technology, 1970, ch. 5.

DEPARTMENT OF EDUCATION & SCIENCE, Design Note 5, *The School and the Community*, Architects & Buildings Branch, 1970.

Education Pamphlet No. 57, *Towards the Middle School*, H.M.S.O., 1970, ch. 5.

Reports on education No. 66, *Trends in School Design*, H.M.S.O., 1970.

COUNCILS AND EDUCATION PRESS LTD, *Consortia '71*. A supplement published with the 30 April 1971 issue of *Education*.

SEABORNE, M., *The English School: Its Architecture and Organization 1370–1870*, Routledge & Kegan Paul, 1971.

Index